W9-BBW-171

THE RIGHT BOAT FOR YOU

THE RIGHT BOAT FOR YOU

Bill Robinson

HOLT, RINEHART and WINSTON

New York · Chicago · San Francisco

Published simultaneously in Canada by Holt, Rinehart
and Winston of Canada, Limited.

Library of Congress Cataloging in Publication Data

Robinson, William Wheeler, date
  The right boat for you.

   1. Boats and boating. I. Title.
GV775.R62 1974   797.1   73–16243
ISBN 0–03–012246–5 (cloth)
ISBN 0–03–088388–1 (pbk.)

First Edition

Designers: Mary M. Ahern and Helene Berinsky
Printed in the United States of America

Contents

Preface

In the complexities of modern life, recreation and the constructive use of leisure time are vital to the well-being of society. Through involvement in a rewarding, enriching pursuit, an individual becomes a more positive person, well-rounded and stamped with the character of a "doer," breaking out of the mold of inert acceptance and passivity that often seems the easiest solution to handling the pressures of our times.

There are few such pursuits that offer better opportunities and a more pleasant challenge of involvement than boating. In its many facets of sail and power on all kinds of water, it has something for almost everyone. From the laziest kind of "put your feet up and have a beer in the sun" sort of relaxing to the demands of ocean racing, it offers a vast world of opportunities for every type of talent and temperament, and for individuals of all ages and physical abilities, with both sexes equally able to enjoy participation.

For some, a boat is only a casual part of the whole recreational picture. For others, it becomes a way of life, with an important effect on habits and life styles. Boating is a great recreation for families, particularly.

Although the joys of boating are subjective—and sometimes even spiritual or poetic—there has to be a practical approach to the purchase of a boat. This is, then, a practical book on how to choose and buy a boat, based on almost 50 years of that subjective enjoyment of boating.

Rumson, N.J.
January 1974

BILL ROBINSON

1

The First Steps

Which is the right boat for you, and how do you go about selecting and acquiring it?

Walk into the store and buy one, you say. That is, naturally, the ultimate step, but there are steps leading up to it that should be followed properly, or the boat you end up with may be the wrong one, a source of frustration and disappointment. On the other hand, if you have done your homework correctly, the right boat can bring endless pleasure and satisfaction.

Individual circumstances and considerations point to the answer. Over the years, in my case from adolescence through the normal stages of marriage and family life to middle-aged contemplation of retirement in the not too distant future, the boats that suited me at particular moments make up quite a list. It started with a 16-foot daysailer sloop of indeterminate origin that was bought for $35 and never, in the time I had her, remained afloat for more than 24 hours without pumping. After that came an 18-foot cabin sloop, a 19-foot cabin sloop, a 22-foot cabin cruiser, a 13-foot Boston Whaler outboard, four different one-design racing sailboats, a 24-foot cruising auxiliary sloop, an 18-foot Cape Cod catboat, and a 36-foot tri-cabin cruising auxiliary sloop. (Assorted prams and dinghies are not included, though the ownership of one, or of a canoe or small cartopper outboard, can be a momentous step in influencing a family's recreational habits.) The list runs the gamut from $35 to $35,000, and as it shows, we have crossed over the line between power and sail several times.

Why do people own boats in the first place? The reasons are complex and governed by many considerations. There was even one boat manufacturer (since gone broke) who felt that there was absolutely no logical reason for anyone ever to own a boat, and he therefore based all his sales promotions and ad campaigns on an appeal to emotion pure and simple. In a way, he had a point. All forms of recreational pleasure are based on an emotional appeal that is actually an important element of the quality of one's life. But then, especially in the case of boating, logic and reason of some sort must follow.

The first choice between power and sail may come down to some very simple circumstances, such as being located on a lake that outlaws powerboats, or on a narrow, hill-girt river impossible for sailing. It would seem obvious that no one would base a deep-water sailing vessel on a mountain lake or go offshore for sport fishing in a canoe, though it is amazing how often the most unlikely vessel turns up on a given body of water, simply for reasons that happen to suit the owner.

Eagle Mountain Lake near Fort Worth, Texas, less than 5 miles long and with no outlet to any other body of water, is home base for a fleet of auxiliary sailboats up to 40 feet long and fully capable of heading for Bermuda. They are raced on the tiny lake, and are used for picnics and daysailing, because large powerboats are not permitted.

On another lake near there, not much larger but with no restrictions on boat type, a dealer handling a well-known line of stock power cruisers and motor yachts recently had the heaviest one-year volume in the country for boats of that type among any of that company's dealers. This aroused the curiosity of the company's sales manager, who thought he should investigate the situation to see whether the dealer was engaging in some under-the-counter discounting to other areas or similar hanky-panky.

Not at all. When the sales manager arrived at the dealer's marina on a cove off the main lake, he was greeted by the sight of acres of glossy cruisers lined up in slips, and he was ceremoniously taken aboard for a day's outing in the largest yacht there, a luxurious 60-footer. The owner had taken delivery a year ago, and as they headed out of the slip there was a great stir and bustle of preparations because they were stopping at the fuel dock for the first time since they'd owned the boat. Her tanks had been filled on delivery, and this was the first time they'd had to take on fuel by themselves in a year of "operations." The usual voyage was of a few hundred yards to an anchorage where they spent the weekend if they went out at all.

These Texas boats are obviously special cases. They are supreme examples of boats as an ego extension, which is not to be overlooked as a major reason for boat ownership, and, as everyone knows, ego extension in Texas is something special.

Ego extension, personal expression, or whatever one might call such individualism, is one reason that people own boats, but there are many others that are more complex. Back of them should be some logic and forethought. There should be analysis of how and why a certain boat should be chosen at a given time. Sometimes the choice is made with all the "logic" that can go into falling in love. Why does a man fall in love with a bad-tempered, buck-toothed girl, or a girl with a potbellied lout? Through the strange chemistry of love, the couple may live happily ever after, but falling in love with the wrong boat is almost certain to lead to unhappiness and incompatibility. The chemistry doesn't work quite the same way.

To give an idea of how the thinking should work, here's how it went for a few of the boats we have owned.

The first one, that leaky sloop, was simply a question of the price being right. Not much else was, and $35 was about all I could manage just out of college in 1939. I did get my money's worth of sailing out of her (and even sold her for $40 when I went into the Navy a few years later).

The 18-foot daysailer was our first postwar boat, when our family numbered four with Robby age 4, Martha 2, and Alice on the way. This boat, bought used, was well suited for our situation, with shallow draft, a necessity on our home waters of the Shrewsbury River in New Jersey, a small inboard engine to handle the swift local tides, an easily managed rig with self-tacking jib, a big cockpit, and a cuddy cabin where the kids could nap or play house. She was ideal for casual daysailing and for beaching on an island for a picnic or marshmallow roast, which we often did to keep the sailing hours from exceeding the attention span of the kids. The price was right, too—about $500. Perhaps today a similar buy would be several hundred dollars more.

The 22-foot outboard cruiser was selected when the children were 12, 10, and 7. This is a great age range for family outings—a day of fishing, a sightseeing trip, a swimming picnic. The kids wanted wider horizons than the daysailer provided, but with the mobility and flexibility of power. It was also a great adventure to spend a night on the boat. She was pretty small for this, but we could just manage by using an air mattress for Alice. The boat was advertised as a "four-sleeper" and she was, even though there wasn't room to stow a toothbrush, much less a change of clothes, and if the adults didn't mind "hanging ten" about a foot out into space from the bunks. Sleeping aboard was such a treat that the kids even did it in a nautical version of a pajama party with the boat tied up in the slip.

In that era Robby and Martha, the two eldest, were also involved in one-design racing at the local sailing club, in a Comet and Wood Pussy respectively, and the cruiser was a good parental spectator and kibitzing craft. She had her limitations, but she did fit in with the family's activities at the time. The one-design racing (plus Little League, swimming races, and all the usual involvements at that age) kept us close to home, so there was no need for a cruising boat with longer range. The boat we had was strictly an overnighter, but that was enough.

A very important addition a year or two later was the Boston Whaler. This distinctive outboard runabout has been a teen-age status symbol since it first came out, and it was the most prized vessel in our fleet for a while. It gave the kids great freedom and mobility in getting around among the sailing club, beach, and friends' houses; saved mother countless miles of jitneying; taught the children respect for things mechanical (plus the thrill of operating something mechanical while below auto-driving age) ; and gave them a new activity, water-skiing. I got to ride in the Whaler about twice in the three years we owned her, since she was preempted on teen-age duty most of the time. All in all, she was about as successful a boat, at the time we had her, as has ever been in the family.

Somewhere in this period the urge to own a cruising-racing auxiliary began to build in me. There had been no point in trying to operate one when the children were small, or when they were wrapped up 150 percent in club racing, Little League, and similar involvements. But as they moved into their midteens, their horizons began to

THE ROBINSON FLEET OVER THE YEARS: (*facing page*) 18-foot daysailer, 13-foot 6-inch Wood Pussy; 9-foot Turnabout, 24-foot Amphibi-Ette

THE ROBINSON FLEET: 13-foot 4-inch Boston Whaler, 13-foot 6-inch
Blue Jay; (*facing page*) 13-foot 9-inch 420

THE ROBINSON FLEET: 18-foot catboat, 36-foot Morgan Out Island

expand a bit, and they provided a ready-made crew; the time seemed right to go into something bigger.

This was when the question of fitting a boat to the needs of the moment became almost impossibly involved, but we were able to establish certain criteria for what we needed. We wanted a cruising sailboat we could afford that would be shallow draft for home-area operations, sleep five, sail well enough to be competitive, and, since we wouldn't have the time to move her by water to different cruising and racing areas, would be trailable.

When we added all these requirements and then tried to be logical about satisfying them, it looked like an impossible combination. We would almost certainly have to give up on something.

And yet in the back of my mind, there was a long talk I'd had perhaps ten years previously at the National Motor Boat Show in New York with a boatbuilder from Maine named Farnham Butler. He was an ardent missionary for light-displacement, reverse-sheer cruising boats as a solution to the problems of space and cost. I had listened to his pitch carefully, and it had been stashed away in my subconscious ever since. I knew that he was still building boats (which he first called Controversies because so many people had trouble adapting to reverse sheer and light displacement) and I sent for the literature for his smallest model, a 24-footer called an Amphibi-Ette. After careful study she turned out to fill every one of our requirements. Sleeping five was a bit of a squeeze, but given the age of our children, 15, 13, and 10 at the time, it could be done, and everything else fit: shallow draft, trailability, roominess, sailing ability (we hoped, for all this had to be taken on faith from secondhand reports) , and, most important of all, low cost.

We had really made a careful study of what we needed and what we could handle, and the result, *Mar Claro,* gave us nine years of great satisfaction. She fulfilled every requirement beautifully, and we sold her very reluctantly when we were deep into the college era. We had won some races, had had countless hours of pleasant daysailing on the shallow waters near home, and had cruised in a diversified range of waters that would never have been available to us if she hadn't been trailable behind the family car. A 24-footer, she got around to southern New England, Maine, the Great Lakes, Florida, and the Bahamas. Our careful analysis of what we needed in the way of a boat at the time had paid off.

To get us through those years when life seemed just a succession of tuition bills, we moved back to the daysailing league with an 18-foot modern replica of the Cape Cod catboat named *Polly*. She suited us well in that she was shallow draft, could be raced in a one-design fleet at the sailing club, had a big, roomy cockpit for party sailing, and was easy to take care of. With the younger generation off in all sorts of directions, sailing meant a twosome again, and we could look out of the house at a good breeze, say, "Let's go sailing," and be out there under sail in less than ten minutes. Maximum use with a minimum of fuss was just what we wanted.

And so we have been through all these varying stages of the family Robinson and have now reached yet another. With the younger generation all adult, all self-sufficient, and since we have more time to ourselves, our requirements are different again. We have gone through yet another analysis of what the best boat for us is as of now and have come up with a whole new set of requirements.

As long as we live on the Shrewsbury, draft is a primary consideration. Anything over 4 feet and we can't even use the channels, much less sail around with any freedom. We are not interested in high-pressure offshore racing. We still race the catboat in the local one-design fleet, and this fully satisfies our competitive urges. For ourselves we want a comfortable cruising boat that can absorb occasional visits from our now-grown children and a growing roster of grandchildren but is mainly a comfortable *bateau à deux*. We want to sail but only under an easily handled rig. We want good power and we want diesel. We have been thinking along these lines for several years while casually looking around, chartering here and there, and sailing in other people's boats. Many people at our stage of ownership give up sail and opt for pure powerboat, or perhaps a motorsailer with a small steadying rig. There is much to be said for forgetting the extra complications and the physical effort of sail, but, with sail as our major field of interest, we still want to stay with it for a while.

And so, after a charter cruise on Florida's west coast to test out the features we had settled on as requirements, we came up with a Morgan Out Island 36 cruising sloop. Her hull is adapted from a former racing model, so she sails well and handles easily, yet she has powerboatlike cabin accommodations. A roller-furling jib and small main make sail handling easy, she has a bow chock for the anchor so that it needn't be wrestled onto the deck, and a 40-horsepower diesel gives her good performance under power. We call her *Tanagra* after the Greek figurines of traveling ladies.

So this is our choice of the moment. The way the years have flown since that leaky 1939, $35 sloop, it won't be too long before we are thinking about full retirement, and this should be a good boat for that eventuality.

In this four-decade catalog of Robinson family boats, there may be an indication of how your boat should be selected. The circumstances and conditions of the moment determine one's needs, and they should be carefully analyzed. As suggested by the particulars of our own boat-owning history, here are some of the generalities that must be kept in mind when you are looking for a boat.

First of all, as I have said, you have the basic choice of sail or power. If this isn't predetermined by your location and physical setup, here are some considerations to keep in mind.

Power has obvious advantages. You have more speed, more range in a given time, and more comfort aboard for the size of boat. It is easier to learn to operate a powerboat, though not as easy as some people think. The forces that affect a boat under way are much more complex than those that must be considered in driving a car. There is a tendency for a novice to say, "I can drive a car; what's so different about a boat?"

A car operates on a stable solid, while a boat operates in an unstable fluid. Not only is a boat affected by currents and its own motion as it moves through the water, it is also subject to wind and waves. A boat has no brakes, a fact which can come as a rude shock to an overconfident "floating car driver."

While these forces are more complex in their influence on a powerboat than any that work on an automobile, they are more easily understood and handled in a powerboat than they are in a sailboat. So there is relative simplicity of operation.

Amenities are more readily available in a powerboat. With a built-in source of power, lights, auxiliary power, refrigeration, and other fringe comforts such as TV are more easily provided than in a sailboat. You can be sure of your schedule in a powerboat, and you can cover a great deal more ground in a given time. You have a platform for fishing, and in many cases there is the extra dividend of water-skiing.

For many men (and a few women) there is a fascination

in playing with gadgetry, and a powerboat offers endless possibilities on this score. Some owners are really happier at the dock playing with their gadgets than they are under way. The boat is like a big home workshop. (With certain differences in gadgetry, this can also be true of a sailboat.)

In space per dollar of initial cost, powerboats do better, though this is a broad generality. They usually accommodate more people within a given length, and they can offer better protection from bad weather in most cases.

A new consideration has been injected into the picture by the developing energy crisis that made itself evident as 1973 gave way to 1974. With talk of uncertainties over availability of fuel for recreational use, the question of sail versus power has gained new meaning to many people, and the question of what type of powerboat would best meet the situation has also assumed added importance. Powerboats are not being programmed out of existence by any means and will continue to be a major factor in recreational boating, but buyers have become more aware of design factors that aid in economizing on fuel use and are more sensitive to the need for careful planning of how a boat will be used.

In general, speed is the number one factor in fuel use, especially speed gained by pushing a heavy boat up on top of the water and keeping her there with excessive horsepower. It is worthwhile for the powerboat buyer to ask just how necessary speed really is, and wouldn't a lighter, simpler boat do as well. If speed is still desired, or if elaborate accommodations and weight-contributing accessories are factors, why not buy a displacement hull that would require much less fuel for hours spent afloat; it would not get as far in calm conditions, but might, like the tortoise and the hare, keep going more steadily in a variety of conditions and still give the desired range in practical fashion. Hours afloat rather than miles covered could be the determining factor. Some people might switch to sail after thinking over these factors.

On the sail side, the advantages (to those who consider them advantages) are almost as obvious. Although initial cost per linear foot and per cubic foot of accommodation in cabin boats may be generally a bit higher in sail, operational costs have to be cheaper. No one has yet figured a way to charge for the wind. Your ultimate range can be anywhere in the world if that's where your interests lie.

Sailing has an aesthetic appeal that is lacking in the operation of a powerboat. There is a special quality to the comparative quiet of a sailboat, to the sense of being one with nature, and of conquering it. The challenge of sailing is much more complex. The world's most experienced sailors will tell you that they never stop learning about sailing. New experiences keep cropping up, new nuances of expertise. The basics of sailing are simple and easily mastered, yet there is no end to its challenges. And of course, sailing competition is one of the most complex, involved, and involving sports there is.

These are a few of the things to be kept in mind when making a choice between sail and power. Once that decision is made, there are other questions to consider.

First of all should be cost, and it is very important to realize just what cost means in relation to a boat. There is, of course, the remark made by J. P. Morgan, which is an absolutely obligatory quote in discussing the cost of a big boat. He was asked by a newly rich oil millionaire who wanted to buy a yacht how much it would cost him to run it. Morgan, whose glossy black *Corsair* was perhaps the most glamorous yacht in the world at the time, answered, "You have no right to own a yacht if you have to ask that question."

That was a valid statement in the days of luxury steam yachts and uniformed crews almost big enough to man a battleship, but it is truly the opposite today. It is very important to know exactly what a boat costs, and this takes in several different items. The price tag on the new boat in a showroom or brochure is not the major factor. This gives a starting point only; it is not the final answer. First of all, payments are very much a part of the picture, and more people will want to know how much down and how much per month rather than the stated price.

On the top of the price tag, depending on the type and size of boat, there are freight costs and sales tax to be figured in, and then there is the list of extras—sometimes called optional extras, but you don't have much of a boat if you don't opt for most of them. Sailboat prices seldom include sails or, if auxiliary power is an outboard, a motor. Even the smallest open boat must have safety equipment such as anchor, fenders, lifesaving devices, lines, etc., and the list grows as long as your arm when the boat is a large cabin cruiser or auxiliary.

Then there are operating costs. The owner who is willing to do his own work can control some of these, but not all. Operational costs include fuel, insurance, berthing (or launching) fees, winter storage, repairs, and maintenance.

Lump all these together, and you have a better idea of what a boat really costs. In the chapters to come, we will go over the specific equipment that should go with the different types of boats and also the operating considerations.

In case all this seems too frightening, remember that ownership of a boat can help cut other items out of the budget. A boat can reduce all other expenditures for recreation, vacations, travel, and entertainment. Amounts previously so allocated can be put into the boat column to take some of the sting out of the total.

When you have arrived at a figure for the overall cost of buying and operating a boat that seems to fit your budget, then you should make an accounting of other items to be considered. You've been through power versus sail and overall cost. Next begin to think about what you want out of a boat, and be practical about it. Many a dreamer has bought too big or too elaborate a boat and has been forced to sit in the marina, unable to operate her.

What kind of waters will she be in? How many people will usually be aboard? What are the major uses—fishing, water-skiing, sailboat racing, etc.? What other uses would be pleasant at least part of the time? You have seen how various Robinson family boats were selected with these factors in mind. Make up your own list, analyze it carefully, and then get ready to go into particulars, which we will do in the following chapters.

2

Used Boats

No matter what type of boat you select as seemingly suitable for your own situation, the question of new versus used must be decided. Naturally, bargain hunters are more interested in the used-boat market, and there is a much wider range of prices possible in used boats of the same type than in new boats. Age, basic condition, supply and demand, the seller's financial situation of the moment, and the possibility of bargaining over the price all make buying a used boat a flexible process.

Price is the main consideration, but it is also a fact that a good used boat, well-found and well maintained by a careful owner, can be in better operating condition than a new boat that hasn't had the bugs worked out of it. With modern mass production of all types of boats right up to luxury yachts, quality control can be a problem, and a boat fresh from the factory often has a lot of little things wrong. When an owner has taken pride in a boat and has kept her in good condition with all the little tricks and gimmicks that make operation so much simpler and pleasanter, she can even be enhanced in value over a brand-new boat of the same model. Boats do not deteriorate in book value half as consistently as automobiles. If a boat was owned by the equivalent of a little old lady in sneakers, the value lasts indefinitely. Not all boats are sold because there's something wrong with them. Rather than someone else's headaches, you may inherit the benefits of his thought and care.

There are other good reasons for buying a used boat. A model no longer in production may be just the thing for you, and the only way to get one is in the used market. There is even a good market now for classics. Old models of stock cabin cruisers dating back as far as World War I are very much in demand, and there are clubs organized around ownership of some makes, such as Elco. For aesthetic reasons, or as a home workman, you may want a wooden boat, and it is almost impossible to find a new wooden boat anymore unless you have one custom built. You may want to join a certain sailboat-racing fleet in your area, and only used boats are available in that class.

All these reasons could govern your choice of a used boat. Now how do you go about looking for one?

There are many ways. The simplest and most direct, especially if you are looking for one of those "needs-a-little-work" specials, is to browse around the boatyards. The bargain basement of boat hunting is the little, out-of-the-way yard where owners are allowed to do their own work. Poke down side roads to little creeks in quiet backwaters. Be diffident about your approach. Start a chat with a yard workman if he's not too busy, and he might "just remember" something worth looking at.

Bargain Hunting

Avoid the glossy marina-cum-showroom for this kind of deal. Although late winter and early spring are the natural times for bargain browsing, the best time of all is in the fall, just at the end of the season (if you're in that kind of climate) . Prices are lowest in the fall, and you can see the boat in its most natural state. In the spring a hasty coat of paint may have covered up imperfections or real flaws, and these can be more easily seen when the boat has had a full season of use.

You're on your own in this bargain-basement atmosphere. Don't expect too much. If you are a real novice, try to bring a friend who has had some experience in boat shopping. Don't bite at the first hot bargain. Shop around and compare, and in the process you can pick up valuable experience in what to look for. Chances are the first bargain will still be there after you've looked around awhile.

I was in the bargain-basement league for many years. After all, how much less than $35 can you pay for a sailboat? No one ever guaranteed she would float or anything. She was just there for that price, so I wasn't gypped. I fixed her up enough to make her respectably operational, even if I could never stop that leak around the centerboard. (In old sailboats this is the most likely trouble spot.) The next two boats were also bought this way, both were basically sound, and both were successful, but my one real clunker was acquired in the bargain-basement league and taught me a good lesson. She was a home-built but professionally designed 24-foot ketch with a sound hull, questionable rig, gutted interior, and a rusty pile of old iron that passed for an engine. It was a marine conversion of sorts of an Essex auto engine that had probably seen better days before it left its original home, and you had to be pretty mature to remember an Essex even in 1948.

A mechanic at the yard where I bought her took one look at it and said, "My God! An old ass-aches! Boy, have you got trouble." And I did.

But not only with the engine. The boat seemed a bargain at $500 in '48, and she would have been great for our family if I'd been the type to do the work needed to fix her

Typical boatyards in Milwaukee (Great Lakes), Maine, and (*facing page*) the Bahamas

up. A good carpenter could have rebuilt the cabin interior, which was finished in a combination of antique orange crate and early, delaminated plywood, and a few new fittings would have helped the rig. As for the ass-aches, I'm afraid it was beyond the ministrations of even the most experienced mechanical genius in the world, which I certainly am not. (My mechanically minded father used to say that I couldn't pour water out of a boot if the instructions were on the heel, but I think he was exaggerating a little.)

And so I took a bath with this noble vessel, and the lesson was worth it in convincing me that it was wrong for me to buy a boat that needed major surgery. I'm all right on seasonal maintenance and simple repairs (and I really can get the water out of a boot), but I was never cut out to do big jobs. That's the way we worked it from then on, with happier results. If you don't have the patience or other temperamental attributes for long hours of working with your hands, don't buy a boat that needs a lot of fixing unless you are prepared to pay someone to do it.

Look out for badly rusted or corroded metal parts, wood that won't hold paint, gaping seams, "hogged" hull lines (a break or unsymmetrical change in the line of a curve or straight section), "weeping" fastenings (exposed metal with adjacent corrosion stains) excessively crazed or cracked fiberglass, delaminated plywood or fiberglass, makeshift, homemade-looking wiring or mechanical hookups, and general signs of owner neglect.

So much for the browsing method. Know thyself before following it, and you may come up with the perfect answer. Don't overestimate your ability to do the work in the first blush of your enthusiasm for a bargain. I'll always remember that 24-foot ketch.

Reading the Ads

The next step up the ladder from the yard-browsing routine is the classified-ad route. Most of the pitfalls mentioned above are lurking here, too, but it is a time-saver. I'm talking now about the individual ads in local papers, not the listings placed by dealers, marinas, and yacht brokers.

When you call in answer to an individual ad, ask a few questions about age, where and how the boat was used, and equipment included in the sale. You can probably get some idea of how the boat has been treated by the way the advertiser talks about her.

Many a happy boat-owning career, including mine, has started in one of these forms of the bargain basement, but there are actually much more reliable methods of looking for a used boat if you are not in the rock-bottom price bracket. I said to avoid the marina-showroom type of operation if low price is the major consideration, but it is actually a good, sensible place to go used-boat shopping. A company with a new-boat dealership naturally takes used boats in trade and has to sell them to consolidate the profit on the new-boat sale. The really beat-up trade-ins are either refused outright or unloaded quickly to the backwater-type yard because the dealer doesn't want to clutter up his place with broken-down boats. His used-boat selection therefore should be a fairly good one.

If he is a smart businessman with a reputation to build or uphold, he should be almost as interested in the used-boat buyer as in a new-boat customer. If the sale is successful, the used-boat buyer will probably be in the market for a trade-up himself. If he has been well treated and is pleased with the secondhand purchase, he will very likely come back to the same dealer for his next boat. This is how a clientele is built by the reputable establishments, so don't be embarrassed by starting out as a used-boat customer.

Here again, shop around before deciding. By looking in an area, you can get a reading on the types of boats that are popular and therefore well suited to local use. The going price range will establish itself and is useful as a yardstick. If a boat seems way out of line from the general price range, up or down, there may be a catch in the deal, or you just might be onto a bargain.

In general, it is a good idea to buy where you can also get service. This isn't a must but it's helpful. Sometimes there will be a warranty period, but this isn't widespread with used boats. Even without it, a reputable yard will want to have satisfied customers and should have a positive service policy. Sometimes this breaks down under the stress of the spring fitting-out rush, so don't expect a great deal of hand holding and the full red carpet treatment if you buy a boat in the March–June period in northern areas. Everybody's trying to get things done at the same time, and the pressure on service facilities is terrific.

In areas where berthing facilities are in short supply, some marinas reserve slips exclusively for customers who buy from them, and this could also be a consideration.

If you can't find what you want through browsing the

local yards, reading the local classified ads, and checking dealers' used-boat stocks, there are classified ads in the national boating magazines. At *Yachting* we have learned that our "Swap Chest," a classified column, is very effective. Aside from producing customers for the boats offered, it is also one of the best-read sections of the magazine. It serves almost as a form of gossip column by showing what people are doing and where their interests lie. You wouldn't use it to look for a small rowboat or outboard runabout, but one-design racing sailboats and all forms of cruising boats are cleared through this medium. It also is worth studying as an indicator of prices.

In both these methods you are, as I have said, pretty much on your own, unless you have an experienced friend to guide you. This really doesn't work too well unless you have more faith in your friend's judgment than most people are willing to place. Very often, all the potential buyer wants is someone to talk to. This happens to me all the time because of the nature of my job, and I am constantly being asked for advice by friends and strangers (which is one of the reasons for writing this book). Often, I am asked questions that are impossible to answer without looking at the boat in question, which happens to be up the Miami River or in Castine, Maine, at the moment. Just knowing the model or type and the asking price means nothing. Sometimes friends ask advice about a certain boat and, as has happened, if I advise against the purchase, they finally admit they have already bought it. Or, whatever I say, they go out and buy the boat anyway. This is like being asked by someone what you think of his new wife. What can you possibly say?

Surveyors

A friend may be helpful, but a professional is better. There are two types of professionals who can be of great value to the used-boat buyer, especially one who is thinking of a major purchase of a fairly sophisticated vessel—marine surveyors and yacht brokers. It is very much to your benefit to avail yourself of the services of one or both if you are entering into a substantial deal.

If, on your own, you have found a boat you like but you want confirmation that it is indeed a good buy, the surveyor is the man to turn to. Surveyors can be found through the phone book, through boatyards, through marine insurance firms, and through marine directories. Fees will vary in accordance with the time to be spent on the survey, both in travel and in actual inspection, with the scope of the job, and with the law of supply and demand in a given area. You should expect to pay the same sort of fee as you would to any other skilled professional man for similar time spent.

The surveyor should be independent of any agency interested in the sale; he will then give a completely impartial rundown of the condition of the boat. He will go over the physical condition of the hull, permanent equipment and rigging, machinery, and electrical system. He may not be able to evaluate the potential performance, but this is really not a part of his assignment. Also, with fiberglass boats he cannot pass on the basic integrity of the original hull construction unless there are some obvious signs of failure or bad practices. If there are no surface flaws or cracks, no voids or crazing, and no evidences of shoddy workmanship, he is as much in the dark about the ultimate reliability of the construction as you are. He may know the methods used by a given boatbuilder, and he may have knowledge of his practices from having inspected damaged boats from the same builder, but this is knowledge based on outside experience, not from looking at the boat in question.

The surveyor's report should be believed. He has no ax to grind, but he does have a reputation to maintain.

If there are some imperfections that can be corrected without too much major work, he will say so. Once you have hired him, it is a mistake to go against his judgment. I had one friend, a rather impractical dreamer-type who thought he was good at fixing things up himself, describe to me on the telephone an ancient sloop he wanted to buy, and from the few things he said, I figured he should use a surveyor. He hired one, got a completely negative report, bought the boat anyway out of sentimental perversity, and got nothing but headaches out of her (and very little use). If your mind is made up that way, save the surveyor's fee. Once you hire him, respect his judgment.

Brokers

The yacht broker is also a professional whose experience can be of great help to any kind of used-boat buyer, from the rankest novice to a Bermuda Race veteran. There are brokers in every major boating area, and they also develop their clienteles both locally and nationwide. Through advertising in the national magazines, they attract customers from all areas who are looking for a particular type of boat.

Yacht brokerages maintain extensive lists of used boats being offered for sale with their complete specifications and other information. Some of them also handle new-boat lines as local dealers, and they offer other services such as marine insurance, charter brokerage, and, in some cases, custom yacht design. Their fees are paid by the seller and are a percentage of the selling price, depending on the size of the sale. Their operations can be compared in many ways with those of real-estate agents.

The big advantage of dealing through a yacht broker is that he knows the boats he has listed and can take many of the uncertainties out of boat buying. Once you have given him a good picture of your needs, he goes to work to match them from the boats on his list. A good broker will not try to sell you a boat you really don't want, and brokers don't last long in this highly competitive field unless they are good. Very often, the boats will have been surveyed, and the reports will be part of their files. If a survey has not been made, the broker can arrange one.

When handled through a broker, a sale is consummated correctly, with all the paperwork taken care of and the little details smoothed out.

As I have said, brokers have to be good to last, and most of them are highly reputable businessmen whose livelihood depends on their reputation. There are some signs that might tell you when you've run into a bad one. If he persists in trying to sell you a higher-priced boat than you can afford, he's making a mistake. If he hasn't done his homework and tries to cover up his unfamiliarity with a listing, beware. If a listing is new, or the broker hasn't had time to bone up on a boat's history and characteristics, he should say so at once and offer to find out what he can. Some brokers feel it is not worth their time to handle boats under a certain price range and will tell you so, which is their prerogative, but they are possibly missing out on you as a potential customer for bigger boats in years to come. In general, except for locally based boats whose handling does not require a lot of travel or correspondence, brokers prefer to deal in boats over 30 feet in either sail or power. Under these sizes, you are better off going to a local dealer who takes smaller boats in trade.

These are the ways, then, of looking for used boats, from poking around in local backwaters to dealing through a broker who may find you the boat you want halfway around the world.

If you prefer to start fresh with a brand-new boat, there are different considerations.

3

~~~~~~~~~~~~~~~~~~~~~~~~~~~~~~~~~~~~~~

New Boats

The advantages of buying a new boat are obvious. Starting from scratch with something that's all your own is better, in most cases, than taking on someone else's cares. As I've mentioned, a boat can appreciate in value if her owner is the thoughtful, careful type and can even be better than new. Most cars are traded in because they've begun to give less than complete satisfaction, while boats are often traded or sold due to a change in the owner's circumstances or, most likely of all, to move up to something bigger.

But still, they are used. Certain items will have begun to show wear and tear, and perhaps you don't really like the fabric the former owner's wife chose for the bunk cushions. You can't buy back engine hours, and electrical systems do deteriorate in a maritime atmosphere.

So let's say you've decided that a brand-new boat is the thing for you. What are the recommended procedures for finding the right one? Again we'll be talking in generalities and basics, with the particulars of different types saved for later chapters.

Buying a new boat can be as simple as walking into a showroom and saying "I'll take one of those," or it can be the lengthy, involved, and often fascinating business of arranging for the design and construction of a custom-built yacht—working with a naval architect.

Bargain Hunting

Starting with bargain hunting as we did with used boats, the procedures are quite different in the case of a new boat. It is possible to "work a deal" by shopping around, but the important consideration is to be sure that the deal really is a bargain and not a disguised rooking. You must evaluate the total picture in making the decision. What equipment is included in the sale? What kind of service will you get after taking delivery? If a trade-in is involved, is the trade allowance a fair one? If you buy from a non-waterfront operator, will you be able to get a berth for the boat at a marina? In the case of a trailable boat, are you being forced to buy a make of trailer you don't want? What kind of resale value does the boat have in your area? If it is an outboard boat, is a brand of motor you may not want forced on you as a package? These are just a few of the questions to ask yourself as you examine a deal for a new boat.

If you are buying a stock boat, the best time for true bargains is at the end of the season, just before models change. The boating industry has developed along the same lines as the automobile industry in changing many models every fall, and dealers with the previous year's models still on hand often put on a special sale in late summer. The disadvantages of this are the lost boating time in early summer and the fact that there will be fairly quick depreciation of the boat soon after buying it when the new models come out. This is not as pronounced as in the auto industry, however, for a boat holds its value longer if well cared for. Also, there is not quite the compulsion in the boating field to be right up to date with the latest model. They don't change that radically. Generally, the yearly model change is more a factor in small outboard boats and motors. Builders do bring out new yearly models of larger boats to bolster sales, but larger cabin cruisers and auxiliary sailboats usually have a model life of several years. If the boat you are looking for is in this category, it is particularly helpful to shop around for special sales. These depend largely on the dealer's circumstances at the moment—whether he has too much inventory, whether he needs cash, whether a competitor is bothering him. If it is truly a sale and not a come-on, a reduced price should be meaningful if the model is staying in production for years more.

Unless the bargain you get by extensive shopping around is a really significant one, my general advice is to deal with the local outlet for the kind of boat you want, if possible. The follow-up on the sale in service and the other benefits of a long-term relationship should outweigh a temporary bargain. This isn't as strong a consideration if there is a good local yard for storage and repairs that is not tied in with a new-boat dealership—a yard whose only business is service—but dealing locally is generally a good idea.

Shopping for a new boat can be a long, drawn-out process (like the time, close to ten years, it took me to decide on the 24-foot sloop we eventually bought). Actually, this period of dreaming and planning can be an exciting time. Anticipation itself is a pleasant emotion, and the thought of a new boat can be savored through many months. (It is when the delivery date passes and delays build up that anticipation tends to turn a bit sour.)

Studying ads in boating magazines, writing in for brochures and poring over them, and visiting showrooms are all part of the fun.

Boat Shows

Boat shows offer a whole anticipatory world of their own and, the way shows are now scheduled, visiting them can virtually be a year-round pastime. The combination of in-water shows in the fall and the big indoor shows in the winter enables one to study boats in their element as well as hauled out with their underwater lines revealed. It is helpful to see boats both ways, and you might also be able to arrange a demonstration ride—always recommended when possible.

Shows are worth the price of admission. (It's a pretty good trick to make the exhibitor pay to display his wares and the buyer pay to come shopping, but it usually works.) This is concentrated comparison shopping, with a chance to see a wide range of makes in a few hours. There may be some waits in line and some crowding in getting aboard, and it can be difficult to get a clear idea of a boat's accommodations with a dozen or so people in her cabin, but these are minor drawbacks. You may become so enthused that you decide to buy right off the exhibit floor, with the major attraction of a possible reduction in price: the exhibitor may want to save the expense of shipping the boat back to the plant and may be willing to make a deal. The boat will be a bit shopworn after all the public attention, and it would be advisable to make sure that there has been no real damage—just superficial wear and tear.

Ask questions at boat shows. Talk to everyone you can and listen to the questions other people ask. They may bring up a point you hadn't thought of. Among the obvious excesses of the sales pitch, there will be kernels of real information. Let it be known that you are interested in a certain competitor's model and see what the reaction

Indoor boat shows in San Francisco and (*facing page*) New York, and an in-water show at Annapolis, Maryland

is. Naturally, the competitor will be knocked, but there might be some meat in what's said. Kick the subject of price around, ask about extras and options, and you should be able to pick up valuable guidelines.

Boat shows are also valuable for investigating equipment, gadgets, and just about every service in the trade. Almost everything that goes into a boat can be found at the major shows, and helpful information on the operation of all the equipment can be obtained by chatting with the company representative. Don't miss the chance to take in a show as part of the process of looking for a boat. New York, Chicago, Boston, San Francisco, Seattle, Los Angeles, and Miami have major shows in indoor arenas in the January–March period, and in-water shows in the fall have become popular in such areas as Stamford, Conn.; Newport, R.I.; Florida; and Annapolis, Md.

Buying from the Builder

So far we have been talking about stock boats on display at shows and readily available in dealer showrooms and boatyards. This can apply to all types of boats from the smallest prams and cartoppers through outboard and inboard runabouts, small daysailers, and one-design sailboats to good-sized cabin cruisers and auxiliary sailboats; but your needs might be special enough to require a further search.

For such needs, there is a wide variety of boats in both sail and power available by direct sale from builders. These are often local yards building on a limited scale, but many of the good ones place ads in the national boating magazines and commercial fishing magazines and papers. They may only turn out a limited number each year and may only place a small ad in one magazine, so diligent study is needed to find a boat in this way. This is no deterrent to the true boat lover who always enjoys a line-by-line perusal of boat ads and articles. At *Yachting,* we find that many readers save back issues for months until they have read them thoroughly and have had a chance to investigate and compare a great many models. This is particularly true for the big boat show issues.

Following up the ads may require considerable correspondence; and if you can possibly manage it, a visit to the yard for a firsthand inspection and perhaps a demonstration ride is advisable. This was more or less the way we acquired our 24-foot Maine-built sloop. One advantage of dealing directly with the builder is the chance to work out customized items. I made one trip to Maine, sat in the bare shell of the hull visualizing layout details, had a day-long conference with the builder, and from then on had a much more personal feeling about the boat, an involvement far different from making first acquaintance with your boat in a showroom.

A stock boat built on an assembly line by mass production methods for sale by dealers cannot be changed. If a builder permitted changes, he would soon go broke. So the only choices available are a number of standard options that do not interrupt the flow of production. While our Out Island 36 was being built, the only chance we had for personal choice was in the number of stock options to be added, such as type of steering, type of hatches, number of ports, lifelines, and stanchions, and that sort of thing, as well as the choice of colors for curtains, bunk cushions, and cabin carpets. These were offered in an ingeniously designed book that had a cutout of the boat's layout in plan view. This could be placed over the different color combinations available for a graphic demonstration of their effect and of how they harmonized with other elements. But aside from such options, it is hard to change so much as an ashtray in a production-line boat.

Not so the individually built boat from a smaller yard. Once you have located what you want, you can then consult on a variety of items, including decor, placement of fixtures, and sometimes even the basic layout. This does not apply solely to larger cabin boats. There are builders of stock powerboat hulls who will install a layout that goes from a bare utility setup for a club launch or day-fishing boat to a variety of layouts suited to different kinds of fishing and cruising. An operation like this is more usually found in areas where workboats suitable for local waters are built, such as Maine, Nova Scotia, Chesapeake Bay, the Carolinas, the Gulf Coast, and the Pacific Northwest.

There are fewer opportunities to buy semi-stock sailboats in this way, but diligent search may still turn one up, again in areas that still support local yards as opposed to mass production manufacturers. And should your preference still be wood as a construction material, this is about the only way to get a new boat built by this age-old method. Mass producers just don't use it anymore.

Foreign Boats

Before the devaluation of the dollar in the early 1970s along with inflation in Europe, buying a boat abroad was a prevalent practice and worthwhile from the money angle. With foreign labor so much cheaper than American, foreign boats were priced well below comparable ones from U.S. yards, even after shipping costs and import duties.

The situation changed as the dollar gap closed, but foreign firms with established reputations have continued to build for export to the U.S. Canada of course has maintained a strong position as a close neighbor with very similar tastes and marketing problems. Farther afield, England, Scandinavia, and Hong Kong have been particularly active; France, Germany, Holland, Japan, and a few other countries have had lesser roles.

There are different categories of foreign boatbuilding. In some areas, notably Hong Kong and Scandinavia, American marketing firms have developed stock designs by American naval architects aimed specifically at the American market. These are sold through dealers, and the result is very similar to buying a domestically built boat through a dealer. The point of origin just happens to be abroad. In some countries stock boats developed for the local market are also sent to America and handled by dealers. Foreign builders sometimes advertise in American magazines and conduct their sales from abroad, and then there are custom boats handled through the naval architects that design them, either American or foreign.

In general, the advantage of buying foreign still hinges on saving money, and this is particularly true for larger, custom-built boats. Stock boats developed for foreign markets may not always suit American tastes.

There is little difference between buying a foreign-built stock boat through American dealers and buying an American-built one. The risk on the buyer's part is small, as his contact is all through American sales people. But the buyer who deals directly with a foreign builder should be very knowledgeable and experienced (and probably patient). In matters of equipment and accommodations that might not suit American tastes and the red tape of having a boat imported, there is a potential for headaches and complications. It is much better to have these taken care of professionally, as a dealer who represents a foreign builder is set up to do. If there is something wrong with a boat, or even in the matter of routine service, obtaining satisfaction from a foreign builder is a long, drawn-out problem for the individual owner.

The best way to have a custom boat built abroad is to

deal through a naval architect who is accustomed to the procedure. In some cases he could be from the country where the boat is built, but many of the top American yacht-design firms have specialized in this and are experienced in giving full service.

Naval Architects

Working with a naval architect is the most sophisticated method of having a boat built, and the ultimate advance up the ladder in boat buying from the simple act of walking into a showroom and saying, "I'll take one of those."

It is the most costly method of buying a boat, as the architect's fee is added on top of the construction cost. There isn't much sense in going to a yacht designer unless the boat is a fairly elaborate and sophisticated one. The fee is well earned, however. The owner's requirements are the working basis of the whole process and his interests are represented at all times. Yacht designing is a sparsely populated profession that provides a living for a mere handful of men in each generation. The best way to locate an architect is, again, through the boating magazines. This is where they advertise, often in conjunction with a yacht brokerage firm that handles used boats and charters. The magazines also print plans of their boats as a regular editorial feature. Boats are often identified by a reference to their designers in write-ups of races and cruises or in articles featuring new boats, and it is possible to gain an impression of a designer's style and his effectiveness through reading this material. Some designers specialize in one type of boat, sail or power, racing or cruising, high speed or offshore, character boats, etc., while others are as diversified as the sport itself and can turn out almost any kind of vessel.

It is possible to turn the whole project over to the

designer, or the owner may participate as his interests dictate. Simply saying, "Build me a boat to win the Bermuda Race for x dollars," or "Build me a motor yacht to sleep six for use in southern waters" can be enough direction for the designer if that's the way the owner wants it. The designer will then take over all decisions on major concepts and minor details, and the owner will eventually step aboard a completed boat.

More often, however, the owner wants to go over many of the items in person and will hold frequent conferences with the designer. A reputable designer will not permit an owner to specify unsound features, and should point out why they are unsound, but the owner's needs and wishes are very much the governing considerations.

One thing to remember is that the more items changed while the boat is being built, the higher the final cost, and the longer the time to finish the job. Unlike the case of stock production-line boats where nothing can be changed, the owner has flexibility but pays for it.

Anyone dickering for a new boat must learn to live with delays and disappointments. Unless the boat is right in the showroom and ready to operate at the moment, there is every expectation that the first date for delivery will not be met. Unfortunately, the whole boating industry, from production line to local boatyard, is notorious for not getting work done on time. It is maddening and frustrating for the buyer and something of a black eye for the industry, but the realistic buyer should make up his mind at the start to expect this sort of thing.

4

⚜️🐍🐍🐍🐍🐍🐍🐍🐍🐍🐍🐍🐍🐍🐍🐍🐍🐍🐍🐍🐍🐍🐍🐍🐍🐍🐍🐍🐍🐍🐍⚜️

Construction Methods

Why are different materials used in boatbuilding, and what are the reasons for choosing one over another? The considerations that govern the choice of construction material include cost, strength, ease of maintenance and repair, and adaptability to the type of boat.

The factors that govern the cost of a boat depend basically on its size. In small open boats the price of the raw material combined with the amount of labor needed to work it make up the major item. In medium-sized boats the weight of the finished boat is an almost infallible indicator of the total cost. In larger boats, 40 feet and up, the basic hull cost is a relatively minor factor; the bulk of the total cost will come from the labor needed to put all the elements of the boat together, plus the wealth of equipment and fittings required to operate an elaborate boat.

For centuries, with labor relatively cheap and very little choice of practical boat-construction materials, the question was simple: what type of wood construction would be best? Then all that changed in the "fiberglass revolution" which started slowly in the 1940s, gathered steam in the fifties, and took over in the sixties. It came at different times to different types of boats, starting with small outboards and spreading gradually to larger boats in both sail and power.

When I ordered *Mar Claro* in the fall of 1957, wood was still the dominant material for auxiliary sailboats. There was hardly any selection in fiberglass, so it was a matter of choosing a wooden boat in sheet plywood, molded plywood, carvel planking, lapstrake planking, or strip planking. She had a strip-planked underbody and coated plywood topsides, a fairly rare type of wooden construction that required no maintenance beyond painting. When I sold her in 1967 she was, as a wooden boat, in a distinct minority, and it would have been difficult to find a new wooden boat to replace her, especially in that size range. Even the replica of the classic Cape Cod catboat with which we replaced her was a product of the fiberglass age —new methods for old traditions.

Today there are several construction methods available, and modern technology is sure to develop still more materials for boatbuilding. Someday we may be floating around in boats made from pressed lettuce leaves or some new form of chemical plastic with wondrous properties yet unimagined. In fact, one manufacturer is now using two thermoplastic materials, ASB plastic and Dylite expandable polystyrene, to build small sailboats.

Before leaving wood in limbo, however, we should have a quick rundown of the various methods of building with it, and their special properties and characteristics. Used wooden boats will be around for a long time (and they are even becoming collector's items) and there no doubt will continue to be a few custom-built wooden boats turned out in odd, traditionalist corners where labor is still cheap.

Wood

CARVEL
This was the way Noah built the Ark—long planks or strakes fitted with edges flush over an interior framework

based on a sturdy keel. The frames can be sawed to shape, steam-bent, or, as is still done in the Bahamas and in other areas where native workboats are built from local woods, selected from the natural shape of trees. Planks can be steam-bent to fit the curve of the hull or hand-bent over frames, depending on the angles and curvature of the hull. Where plank ends meet, a butt block provides backing strength.

Because of wood's natural tendency of swell and shrink according to moisture content, the seams between the planks have to be sealed with some kind of flexible material. Caulking cotton and putty has been the traditional method for centuries, though modern synthetics that seal while stretching have also come into use.

Carvel construction is strong but not in proportion to weight. It allows complex hull forms but does not take highly skilled labor for the basic work, though there is an art to certain phases of it. Maintenance has always been the big drawback for yacht owners, as caulking seams is a very special type of headache (and backache and neckache).

This method developed when man needed bigger boats than could be made by digging out one big log, and it has lasted for uncounted centuries. Native cultures will continue to carry it on in areas where wood is cheap and accessible, labor is cheap, and modern technology has not had an impact.

LAPSTRAKE
This method does not date to Noah, only to the Vikings. The frames are lighter and closer together, steam-bent, and the planks, or strakes, instead of being flush at the seams are lapped over, like the siding of a clapboard house. The Vikings used to tie the planks together, but the modern method of fastening them is either with rivets or screws.

Sometimes a compound is used to improve the seal, but woods like cedar form a good lapstrake fit without a sealant. It is light construction for its strength and does not require caulking. It is relatively easy on maintenance until a boat is old enough to loosen up and work. Then it is almost impossible to prevent leaks. Scandinavian fishermen introduced the method to the U.S., particularly along the Jersey coast, and it spread from there. There is a performance plus from lapstrake in the slight lift and directional stability provided by the laps, with their tendency to turn spray down. Another name for lapstrake is "clinker built."

Molded plywood

Laminated layers of plywood molded in shape under heat or pressure provide strength, lightness, ease of maintenance, and the opportunity for sophisticated forms at fairly low cost. The advantages are similar to fiberglass with less impact strength and more maintenance problems. Molded plywood at one time was competitive with other wood methods but suffered greatly from the fiberglass revolution.

Sheet plywood

This is the home builder's delight and it is still possible to buy kits for building small prams and outboards from plywood. Exterior grades must be used or there will be quick delamination. Sheet plywood, moderately strong if well maced, is only adaptable to simple hull forms without complex surface curves. *Mar Claro*'s topsides were plywood coated with a cellulose fiber plastic and they rivaled fiberglass in smoothness and ease of maintenance.

Sheet plywood is still used extensively for bulkheads and other interior work and is thoroughly accepted for the purpose.

TYPES OF WOOD CONSTRUCTION: lapstrake, carvel, molded plywood; *(facing page)* strip, sheet plywood

STRIP PLANKING

In this method, planks formed as thin strips, usually square or close to it, are edge-glued and then through-fastened with screws or nails. The result is great strength for the weight and fine adaptability to complex hull forms, plus very little maintenance. It would probably have been more popular in wood's heyday except that it is especially time-consuming in labor. *Mar Claro's* strip-planked underbody never leaked a drop in the nine years we had her and required no maintenance beyond painting.

Aluminum

While not used by as many builders, aluminum accounts for almost as many units as fiberglass because of its popularity for small cartoppers mass-produced by a few big companies. These and small runabouts are turned out in great numbers, but there is then quite a jump to the next area of usage which is large, custom-built auxiliaries and motor yachts.

Problems of the period immediately after World War II when inexperienced builders, rushing to get in on the postwar market, used unsuitable alloys for marine construction have disappeared. Corrosion due to this misuse was wrongly attributed to all aluminum, but there is no excuse for it today. Aluminum corrodes only when it is placed in contact with steel, bronze, or copper without proper insulation.

Aluminum has great strength for weight both structurally and on impact, is relatively corrosion-free when handled correctly, and is therefore low on maintenance. It does not even have to be painted except for antifouling purposes. It can be formed into rather complex curves and can be worked quickly and simply with the proper equipment. For this reason it is competitive in cost in small, simply built, mass-produced boats, but it is a luxury material above this category because of its high price. This accounts for its absence in the medium-sized range. In large sophisticated auxiliaries and motor yachts where hull cost is a comparatively small part of the total price of the boat, its excellent properties again make it worth using. Aluminum has also become the standard material for sailboat spars.

Ferrocement

On a visit to New Zealand in 1967, I was taken to see a "new kind of boatbuilding." I had heard vaguely of "concrete boats," and there had been some freighters built of the material during the emergency shipbuilding program of World Wars I and II, but it was still surprising to drive into a small boatyard and see a workman in rubber boots mixing concrete on a wooden platform in front of the shop.

"What's that, the planking?" I asked, thinking I was being funny.

"No, it's the engine bed," was the straight-faced answer, as he continued to shovel away.

There are variations in the method generally called ferrocement, but I won't go into the technicalities here. Basically, it is an inexpensive construction method for boats from about 30 feet and up, where weight is not a consideration. It would not do for an ocean racer or a powerboat designed for fast planing performance, but it is suitable for heavy, rugged cruising and utility boats. The results are often a bit rough as to surface texture, especially on the inside, though it is possible to achieve a smooth glossy finish with good workmanship and proper care.

In this method, concrete is troweled into a mesh of chicken wire set up in the shape of the hull over a pipe framework, and the concrete is then cured to harden. Steam is used in the curing in most cases.

The major advantage is low cost of materials, and much of the labor can be done by relatively unskilled hands. For this reason, it has become the favorite of some back-yard home builders, but it still must be done carefully and correctly or there will be problems of corrosion and deterioration in the metal frame and mesh.

Fiberglass

This is now virtually the standard boatbuilding material, with only aluminum in contention numerically because of its use in mass-produced small boats. By far the greatest number of builders now use fiberglass, and it just about has the market locked up in everything from medium-sized powerboats and daysailing sailboats through middle-sized cruisers and auxiliaries up to the top luxury class.

There are various methods of manufacturing fiberglass boats. Basically, layers of glass cloth, or roving, are impregnated with resin that cures and hardens to form a strong, impact-resistant material that can be molded (before curing) to almost any shape desired. The molding can be done by hand layup over a simple framework or in very costly precision-made molds, depending on the type of boat and the number to be produced. There are also different methods of using the fiberglass layers. An inexpensive method is to spray chopped cloth into the resin. Some builders use layers of fiberglass with a hollow core that is filled with balsa or plastic foam, or bats of fiberglass similar to strip planking in wood.

Fiberglass is not cheap as a raw material, but it can be worked by unskilled labor in less time than a similar wooden structure can be put together, so there is a saving in cost of labor. If it is handled correctly, it is a very durable material that has all the properties required for boat-building.

Mold for a fiberglass hull

There are some misconceptions about fiberglass. It is not completely maintenance-free, and it is not, as some novices expect at first, antifouling when immersed. The bottoms of fiberglass boats must be coated with antifouling paint just like any other material, unless the boat is dry-sailed—stored on land and in the water only when actually being used. Topsides do not require painting, as the gel coat, the glossy outer coat of resin, serves the same purpose as paint and can be impregnated with color. If this surface isn't cared for, however, it will fade and become dull and dirty looking after several seasons. It should be cleaned and waxed periodically; eventually, it may have to be painted to bring back its looks. Impregnated colors do fade, especially bright, solid ones. If possible, they should be protected from the sun with a cover or by changing the direction of mooring—bow one way one time, the other way the next time, if in a slip—so the sun doesn't hit the same side all the time.

Between *Mar Claro* with her coated plywood topsides that were painted once a year and her strip-planked underbody coated with antifouling once or twice a year, and *Polly,* our fiberglass catboat, there was very little difference in time spent on maintenance. The catboat's topsides need cleaning as often, if not more often, than the plywood needed painting.

One problem with fiberglass from an owner's point of view is that it is almost impossible to tell whether the construction is sound and strong. Knowing the method used to lay up the hull can give some reassurance, but even thin, shoddy fiberglass work looks all right in the showroom or marina slip. One has to take its sturdiness pretty much on faith and the builder's reputation.

Until something better comes out of the test tube, however, a fiberglass boat is it for the majority of boat buyers.

Other Materials

We have covered all the major boatbuilding materials, though it is possible to run into a rare example that isn't wood, aluminum, ferrocement, or fiberglass. Steel has been used in pleasure-boat construction in very limited ways, mostly for larger craft. It is too heavy for most small boats and is fairly expensive and difficult to form into the complex surfaces used in many designs. It is of course very strong, but it represents a difficult maintenance problem for the average owner. Once rust is allowed to start, the battle to keep ahead of it is never-ending. Early in the century, bronze was used in building some big luxury yachts, but the problems of corrosion between it and other metals and the cost factor soon put it out of contention.

Rubber and rubberlike synthetics like neoprene are popular for inflatable dinghies and utilities. The major advantage of an inflatable is ease of stowing when used as a dinghy for a larger yacht. The technology of inflatables has developed enough so that they are rugged and safe and far from the flimsy "disposable" craft they were once considered. Rubber or coated canvas is also used in the very limited field of folding, small boats, such as kayaks or canoes, and is fine for the purpose.

Plastics other than fiberglass are sometimes used for small dinghies, cartoppers, and utilities, but the properties are about the same as fiberglass as far as the owner is concerned.

Repairs

Any owner, especially one who likes to do his own work or feels he must for reasons of economy, should consider the problem of repairing boats made from the above materials. Wood is the simplest for the home mechanic, and the tools for working it are easier to come by and use.

Aluminum and fiberglass present more problems, but most boatyards are now experienced in working with them. Repair kits and materials are available to the individual owner, and he should have some means of making emergency repairs when possible. Routine seasonal repairs and maintenance can be done by the skilled owner, but more than likely the boatyard should get the job if it is to be done correctly. Patches can be troweled into damaged ferrocement, given the proper materials—usually a professional job.

No matter what material is chosen, some maintenance is required. There is no magic substance that is absolutely maintenance-free, and the responsibility of maintenance is one of the routines of owning a boat.

5

⚜⚜⚜⚜⚜⚜⚜⚜⚜⚜⚜⚜⚜⚜⚜⚜⚜⚜⚜⚜⚜⚜⚜

Functions of Boat Types

Up to this point, we have been talking about general matters, and now we get down to a few specifics on the special functions of different types of boats. It is an old but very true cliché that every boat is a compromise. It is impossible for any one vessel to be all things to all men, or even a few things to all men. Trying for a boat that is roomy, fast, comfortable, seaworthy, good looking, easily handled, strong, light, economical to operate, shallow draft, and inexpensive is like looking for a lightweight elephant. There "ain't" no such animal. Pick first qualities first and make up your mind that you will have to give up some others.

We have been making this compromise with every boat in the family. When we had racing sailboats, they weren't good for daysailing and knocking about. *Mar Claro* was a remarkable study in successful compromises, but no one could call her the most handsome vessel ever built. With our new Morgan 36, *Tanagra,* we have given up all thoughts of racing, even though she does sail well, to concentrate on the other qualities we want—comfort, roominess, ease of handling.

Function should determine a boat's characteristics, and we should now take a look at some of the more popular functions that pleasure boats perform to see what kind of compromise is best for that function.

There are one-function boats for water-skiing or for one kind of fishing; and there are racing boats in sail and power, and, to some extent, pure cruising boats. You don't go fishing in a racing hydroplane, you don't take a weekend camping cruise in a Sunfish, you don't take your aunt sightseeing in a johnboat, and you don't try to win the Bermuda Race in an Out Island 36 like ours.

Most boats have multiple functions. The average outboard runabout can be used for water-skiing, fishing, sightseeing, and overnight camping. It may not be perfect for any one of these uses but it can perform all of them. If you only cared about water-skiing, you might have a high-powered boat with a special cockpit arrangement for handling skiers, but the multipurpose boat can do all right for skiing and then half an hour later be anchored in a good fishing hole.

Auxiliary sailboats used to combine racing and cruising quite well, but there has been a tendency away from this combined function under the increased pressures of deep-water racing competition. Pure cruising boats, in which no provision is made for racing, have developed as a popular type, and the cream of the ocean-racing crop has been refined so far that few allowances are made for cruising amenities.

Larger powerboats, except those with the single function of sport fishing, are relatively versatile. Here the big compromise is in speed versus comfort and economy. Some fast powerboats are comfortable in all but the roughest conditions—and the deep-V hull has had a marked influence here—but there is no way of achieving speed cheaply. Speed means fuel burned and fuel costs money. The big split therefore is between the relatively flat-bottomed or V-bottomed boat that can get up on top and plane at speeds between 12 and 25 knots or more, paying for the privilege, and the so-called trawler-type, displacement hull that chugs along economically at under 10 knots in a more comfortable, easy motion. This latter type is particularly popular for offshore cruising over an extended range and for live-aboard owners, including retireds who are never in a tearing hurry to get somewhere.

The practice of trailing boats behind the family car has brought about a whole new breed of boats in both sail and power. They can have functions as varied as the ones mentioned above but they all are designed to be transported by trailer. Fiberglass was a major factor in the development of trailer boats. When wooden boats of conventional plank and seam construction were left out of water for any period of time, they dried out, opened up, and leaked when first placed back in the water. The seamless wood construction methods, such as plywood and strip and to some extent lapstrake, helped but it wasn't until fiberglass became thoroughly accepted that trailing boats came into their own.

Another factor was the shortage of mooring facilities and berthing slips. When an owner can store his boat in his driveway, backyard, or garage, and then take his choice of different bodies of water each time he decides to get afloat, a tremendous flexibility is added to boat

A 15-foot sport fisherman on trailer

Author's 24-foot *Mar Claro,* a keel-centerboarder, was designed
to be trailed.

ownership. Money is saved, as launching fees are usually
less than slip rentals over a season, and there is no need to
rent a boat on vacation if you can take your own with
you. In the case of boats with accommodations, motel or
hotel costs can also be avoided.

A boat designed for trailing should have certain special
characteristics. The shape of the underbody and light
weight for the size are important factors. A powerboat
cannot have a deep skeg or struts, shafts and propellers
that protrude too deeply, so outboards and stern drives
adapt best; a sailboat should not have much of a keel. A
whole new breed of sailboat has been developed for the
trailing trade, utilizing a principle known as a swing keel
or drop keel. This works like a centerboard but is not
intended for raising and lowering at will while sailing. It

recesses into the hull for trailing and for landing on shallow beaches but is fixed in place for sailing.

Mar Claro was an early type designed for trailing, as her class name, Amphibi-Ette, proclaimed, and the flexibility this gave us greatly increased our enjoyment of the boat. We would never have had the time to sail her all the way to the areas we explored in her, such as the Florida Keys, Bahamas, Great Lakes, and Maine, but by trailing her there we did them in normal vacation time.

Choosing a trailer depends on the type of boat used. Usually there is a package of boat, motor, and trailer. Certain trailers fit certain boat types, and a dealer usually stocks trailers that are suitable for his line of boats. It seldom pays to shop around independently for a trailer.

It does not pay to skimp on trailers and trailer accessories, such as the hitch for the tow car. Again, a dealer is usually set up to equip the car with the proper gear, too, or to recommend someone who specializes in this work. Get the best and strongest hitch and safety chains. A hitch should be attached to the car frame, not just to the bumper, except in the case of the very lightest boats, and the car should also have equipment for braking the trailer and extra shock absorbers for the rear springs when the boat-and-trailer load is heavy enough to require them. The specifics of this vary so much in each case that it is impossible to do more than generalize here but, again, a good dealer should be able to provide the whole package.

Fishing boats range from the little cartopper for a country pond to that most complex type in the whole pleasure boat field, the offshore sport fisherman. In each one the basic function governs every inch of the boat so that it is an efficient platform for hooking and landing fish. All other considerations are subsidiary.

This doesn't mean that you can't fish casually from

almost anything that floats, but the true fisherman wants a boat purely for function number one. Seating and control arrangements, hull configuration, placement of equipment, and interior layout (if the boat is big enough) are all designed with catching fish in mind.

To further define function in a boat, here is a list of boat types and terms that might pop up while you are boat hunting, with a short description of each type's major function, or of the meaning of the term.

Small Craft

Canoe—Light craft propelled by paddling; double-ended in most cases; can be fitted with light motor and sail.

Rowboat—A small open boat propelled by oars; often flat-bottomed and simply built. Sometimes, when called a rowing boat, denotes a boat with shaped hull and lines especially designed for easy rowing as a sport or form of exercise.

Cartopper—A light boat that can be transported atop a car; can be equipped with small motor and/or sail.

Kayak—A double-ended boat, very often foldable for stowage, very light, with minimum sitting space; propelled by a double-ended paddle; sometimes fitted with a small sail.

Pram—A blunt-bowed small boat, reminiscent of a baby carriage in shape, for rowing, small motor, or sail.

Dinghy—General term for a small boat used to service a bigger one, synonymous with tender; can be inflatable or rigid. Sometimes sailing dinghies are used purely as a small racing class. In British Empire parlance, a dinghy is any small racing sailboat.

Power

Outboard runabout—An open boat propelled by outboard motor; can be used for a variety of purposes.

Inboard runabout—Same function as outboard but powered by an inboard motor.

Sport boat—Usually a glossy, fancily finished boat for high-speed joyriding.

Ski boat—A small, maneuverable boat, highly powered for its size, with minimum seating for two, expressly intended for towing water-skiers.

Ski barge—A large, roomy, open boat with high power, outboard or inboard, from which skiers can operate, with room for them to come aboard and for stowage of gear.

Utility—General term for an open, all-purpose boat; often a workboat.

Launch—General term for a small, open powerboat. Usage dates from early days of boating and is not often heard now.

Stern drive—Means of propulsion in which engine is inboard but propulsion unit protrudes through stern and is outside boat. Also called inboard outboard or IO.

Johnboat—A long, narrow boat especially set up for fishing in protected inland waters.

Bass boat—A deluxe, more elaborate version of a johnboat, with swiveled fishing chair high above hull, good power, and special provisions for stowage of fishing tackle and handling of fish. On saltwater a bass boat is a maneuverable open utility especially designed for catching striped bass.

Pontoon boat—A flat platform placed over floats or pontoons; can be open on top, canopied, or have a cabin; usually outboard powered.

Outboard cruiser—A boat with living accommodations, but small enough to be powered by outboard motor or motors. Use of outboard power leaves more room in hull for accommodations and permits trailing more easily.

Cabin cruiser—General term for a motorboat with living accommodations, but usually refers to an inboard powerboat.

Houseboat—A boat with houselike cabin on a flat hull, self-propelled or not.

Flying-bridge cruiser—A boat equipped with a bridge above the main cabin with controls located there for better visibility and greater utilization of outside space; often shortened to "flybridge" in ads.

Trunk cabin cruiser—A boat with the upper part of her cabin protruding above the deck and set in from the sides of the boat to permit passage fore and aft alongside it.

Flush-deck cruiser—A boat whose deck is the overhead for her interior cabin. Another enclosed space called a deckhouse can be placed on top of the deck as well.

Tri-cabin cruiser—A boat with accommodations fore and aft inside the hull and with a higher center cabin in a deckhouse.

Motor yacht—A term to describe a large, luxuriously appointed vessel; no official size limits, just the builder's or owner's options.

Yacht—A yacht is actually any vessel used for pleasure, from a pram on up. Again with no official limits, it

POWERBOATS: cartopper, dinghy,
inflatable dinghy; (*facing page*)
outboard runabout, inboard
runabout, sport boat

POWERBOATS: utility, stern-drive sport boat; *(facing page)* bass boat, houseboat, flying-bridge cruiser

POWERBOATS: flush-deck cruiser, tri-cabin cruiser, motor yacht; (*facing page*) trawler, sport fisherman

is most often used colloquially for larger boats in both sail and power. Yachting as a term takes in the whole sport of pleasure boating in every phase. You may call any boat you own a yacht, rightfully.

Trawler—A husky powerboat with deep, heavy hull similar to a commercial fishing trawler. Roomy accommodations, relatively slow speeds, good seakeeping ability; also referred to as an offshore cruiser.

Sport fisherman—A high-powered, seaworthy boat especially designed for good speeds offshore and long range, with deep-sea fishing as her only function and accommodations only as necessary for the type of fishing; almost always has a flying bridge and often a high tuna tower.

Sail

There are as many sailboat types as there are bodies of water in the world. Local names abound and rig variations and combinations are endless, but the following are the terms most likely to be encountered by today's sailors.

Boardboat—A simply rigged boat with a flat hull, originally based on the design of a surfboard; also called a sailboard. Original commercial name in this field was the Sailfish, which is often used as a generic term.

One design—A sailboat built to certain specifications so that all boats in that class have the same speed potential and are raced without handicap. First boat home wins. There are literally thousands of one-design classes in the world sporting names of animals, birds, fish, celestial bodies, numbers (referring to sail area, in most cases), designers, and geographic locations. Well-known examples include Stars, Snipes, Comets, Penguins, Lightnings, Dragons, 420s, Rhodes 19s,

Blue Jays, Fireballs, Sunfish, Lasers, and many many more.

Daysailer—Usually an open boat intended for nonracing use, but also the name of a popular one-design class (but spelled Day Sailer).

Development class—Boats built within a certain set of measurement limits—but not with exactly similar dimensions like one designs—that race together without handicap. Level racing is a term used for larger boats racing offshore under this system.

Handicap racer—Any boat that races against dissimilar boats under a system of ratings and time allowances to permit boats of unequal size and speed potential to race together. First boat home does not necessarily win. Winner is boat that does best with her time allowance.

Ton classes—Certain measurement limits, permitting variations in design, for boats that race without handicap in level racing. The term "Ton" has nothing to do with the weight of the boat. The first Ton class happened to race for an old trophy known as the One Ton Cup, and various other Ton classes, such as Quarter Ton, Half Ton, Three-Quarter Ton, and Two Ton, have been set up for similar competitions. The names are a purely arbitrary gimmick.

Overnighter—A boat with simple accommodations for sleeping aboard for a night or two under camping conditions, but not full living accommodations.

Auxiliary sailboat—Any sailboat equipped with inboard or outboard power.

Cruising auxiliary—Primarily a sailboat, but with full living accommodations and an engine; often just called an auxiliary.

Sailboats: (*facing page*)
development class (Moth), one
design (Lightning); catamaran,
ocean racer (*upper right*),
motorsailer

Ocean racer—An auxiliary sailboat designed especially for competing in long-distance races offshore, either in the ocean or Great Lakes. Living accommodations are kept to the bare minimum for a racing crew, with few amenities as a rule.

Meter boat—Some racing sailboats are built to an international formula in which various dimensions and weights and sail area are balanced in an equation that must have a certain number expressed in meters as its answer. Best known is the 12-Meter Class boat used in America's Cup competition. Nowhere on a 12-Meter need there be any dimension that is 12 meters.

Motorsailer—A self-descriptive term applying to a boat that has a powerful engine, stronger than most auxiliaries, roomy accommodations, and a relatively short rig. She is supposed to combine the benefits of sail and power. Another term is a 50-50, and the term "full-powered auxiliary" is sometimes used when the balance is a bit to the sailing side.

Tri-cabin—This refers to the same layout in sailboats and powerboats. Usually the boat's cockpit is forward of the after cabin. This type is also called a center-cockpit model or an after-cabin model.

Double-ender—A boat with a pointed, or canoe, stern; can also apply to powerboats, but rarely found in modern types.

Catamaran—Refers to a hull type in either sail or power, though more common in sailboats, in which two hulls are joined by a flat platform deck and/or bracing struts; sometimes shortened to cat, causing confusion with catboats.

Trimaran—A three-hulled boat in which the center hull is generally the largest one.

Rigs

There are infinite variations in rig, but the most commonly seen are:

Catboat—A boat with no headsail forward of the mast, which is placed well in the bow. Usually a single-masted boat but there are cat ketches and schooners (see below).

Sloop—A single-masted boat with a mainsail and a jib, or jibs.

Cutter—A single-masted boat with the mast set farther aft than a sloop's, often with a double headrig. There is no official demarcation between a sloop and a cutter.

Yawl—A two-masted boat with the smaller mast aft of the rudderpost.

Catboat

Boardboat

SPINNAKER

Sloop

Yawl

GENOA JIB
(OVERLAPPING)

Ketch

MARCONI

GAFF

Schooner

Ketch—A two-masted boat with the smaller mast aft but forward of the rudderpost. In yawls and ketches the after mast is called the mizzen or sometimes the jigger. It is usually taller in ketches than in yawls.

Schooner—A boat with two or more masts with the smaller mast(s) forward.

6

〰〰〰〰〰〰〰〰〰〰〰〰〰〰〰〰〰〰〰〰

Small Powerboats

Small powerboats, up to 20–22 feet, make up the largest category of pleasure boats. The outboard runabout, as a general-purpose boat, is the most popular. Within the category there are many basic points to consider and then hundreds of minor variations among individual models. In addition, as we have noted previously, many special-function boats fall into this category, as well as a number of small runabouts and utilities that are inboard powered.

Hull form, layout and arrangements, and power plant are the three major considerations.

Hull Forms

Almost all small powerboats are light-displacement or planing types designed to rise up when in motion and skim over the surface of the water rather than move through the water with underbody submerged. The few boats that have hulls that displace water are designed this way because they are only suitable for a low-powered engine, or because it is more important that they have cubic capacity and weight-carrying ability than speed.

Small prams and dinghies, whose major function is to carry a large number of people for their size for short distances between bigger boats and the shore, should not have high-powered engines. They should operate as displacement hulls and at slow speeds. The two basic forms for displacement hulls are round-bottom and V-bottom and their shapes are just what their names imply. The V-bottom's popularity stems from its ease and cheapness of construction of simple materials such as plywood. It provides greater initial stability in a small boat but is not quite so easily driven through the water as is a round-bottomed hull as a general rule. Nor is the V-bottom's ultimate seaworthiness quite as good, though it usually has more room in it in proportion to overall length. The interior has almost a boxlike configuration.

A round-bottom in a displacement hull is a bit more easily driven (and rows a lot better if oars are the power). It has less initial stability and probably not as much smooth-water carrying capacity, but it should have relatively better rough-water ability.

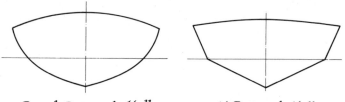

Round-Bottomed Hull   *V-Bottomed Hull*

These characteristics have to be generalized because individual design features can change them in each type —always, as has been pointed out before, as the result of some compromise. Only the very smallest of open powerboats are usually confined to displacement operation, as the motor powerful enough to get them on top of the water would be too powerful for the hull size, shape, and construction.

By far the greater number of small powerboats do get up on the surface and plane, or at least partially plane. There are many variations in hull form to bring about this type of performance. The following are the more commonly seen.

FLAT-BOTTOM
Nothing could be simpler than a plain flat-bottomed hull, and it will skim over the surface if driven by sufficient power. The old-fashioned, familiar rowboat is an example, and over the years there have been boats of all sizes with flat bottoms. The problem of the flat-bottom form is that it is too simple. It has little directional stability, pounds badly in even a small chop, loses stability at high speeds, and lacks construction strength. This was soon evident in the first racing boats that broke away from the displacement principle with flat-bottom design.

The performance of a flat-bottomed hull can be improved with a few simple additions. A skeg or small keel or even a little finlike appendage near the stern will help directional stability. The addition of a small amount of dead rise (a shallow V-form in the hull bottom) in the forward sections will reduce pounding. Some almost flat hulls are rounded at the edges (known as the bilges of the chines) to help reduce pounding and to make them more manageable on turns. A sharp turn in a true flat-bottomed hull can be a dangerous maneuver since the chine will bite in and throw the boat out of control.

THREE-POINT
Some racing powerboats and sport boats of extreme design and performance have what is known as a three-point hull. This is a flat-bottomed hull with extra appendages out on the sides like stubby, down-turned wings, called sponsons. When the boat is at high speed, these lift the boat off the flat-bottomed area of the hull so that only

the sponson tips and the propeller (in the stern) are touching the water. This design is only for expert drivers who are used to controlling boats at high speed. Those who want to get into powerboat racing are a breed apart from the average boat buyer.

V-BOTTOM

As its name implies, this is a bottom with some deadrise. It is a common, popular hull form. The deeper the V, the less likelihood there is of pounding but the more difficulty there is in making the boat plane. Some hulls have a fairly deep V forward that gradually flattens out toward the stern to give them ease of entry in the waves and the lift of a flat bottom aft. Materials that permit some sophistication in hull form, such as fiberglass and aluminum, have allowed the development of many variables on the basic V-bottom. V-bottoms have good initial stability and carrying capacity. However, they lose ultimate stability in a hurry in really rough beam seas and, especially if the stern is very flat, they can also be difficult to control in a steep following sea when they tend to broach (slew sideways and tip sharply). V-bottom boats are sometimes referred to as "hard-chine" boats. There can also be a hull

A hard-chine cabin cruiser

Sport boat with deep-V hull

form that is basically V-bottomed but has the chines rounded off.

Deep-V

This type was designed and developed by Ray Hunt, a versatile New Englander who has turned out everything from small powerboats to ocean racers and America's Cup yachts, and it has had an important effect on power-boat design and performance since the 1950s. The angle of the V is much sharper than in the more conventional V-bottom, and it is carried all the way aft to the transom (the flat planel at the back of a boat). In addition, longitudinal stringers or long thin strips, like small chines, run the length of the hull. This form provided a revolutionary improvement in rough-weather performance at good speeds, dramatized by several wins in heavy going in the Miami–Nassau powerboat race. The entry is soft and nonpounding, and the speed potential is good, helped by the stringers, which also provide directional stability as insurance against broaching. The deep-V design requires plenty of power to get it up on a plane and keep it there, and it is therefore rather high on fuel consumption. However, its benefits in rough-weather performance introduced a whole new dimension in powerboat operation. Some imitations and variations on the Hunt design have not been as successful, but the deep-V is now a well-accepted member of the family of hull shapes.

CATHEDRAL

The type of hull loosely referred to as cathedral—interchangeable with tri-hull, gull wing, and several other names given by individual manufacturers—is that it has all but eliminated the tendency, particularly strong in conventional V-bottoms, to broach in a rough following sea. The cathedral type has a center, V-shaped section of underbody, and then, instead of continuing up in the V-shape to the chines at the outer edges of the bottom, the transverse hull lines reverse down again so that the chine area is another V-shaped or slightly rounded form projecting into the water. These have maximum buoyancy and lift and they tend strongly to prevent the boat from "rolling in," as in the case of a hand-chined V-bottom. The more down pressure applied on them as the boat rolls, the stronger lift they have. The two "tunnels" formed be-

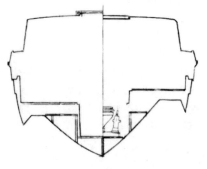

COMPOSITE DRAWING OF CATHEDRAL HULL: midships section on left, bow section on right

tween the inner V and the "wings" of the cathedral chines also help with lift both for stability and for speed performance. Variations in cathedral or gull-wing design can produce soft or hard rides and wet and dry boats, but the most recent developments, with the V of the center section carried deeply all the way to the transom and with a lip around the area under the foredeck, are dry and soft at most speeds in all but the roughest conditions.

Slotted

A later variation of the cathedral type adds a diagonal slot amidships in the center section of the bottom. This is formed by a curving upward of the after section of the underbody rather than a continuation of what would be normal running lines in this area. Two thin sponsons then run forward from the outer edge of the slot to the bow sections. This type of hull has great stability when in motion because the V section in the center pushes the water out into the slot area, like a wave off a normal hull. The water in the slot, which cannot be compressed, then acts as a cushion to give upward lift and stability to the hull and to keep the stern in a good "attitude" toward waves, counteracting the tendency of the bow to swing up too much in going over waves.

Each manufacturer has his own version of these general hull types, but taken together they cover just about every kind of form that the buyer of a small powerboat will encounter.

Arrangements

The layout of the small open powerboat can be much more varied than one would imagine. There has been a tendency to line the seats up like an automobile's. This is fine for some types of joyriding but, depending on the use a boat is to be put to, the arrangement of seats, lockers, and controls can make a great difference.

Because an automobile driver sits in the front seat, many manufacturers who jumped into the boating boom in the 1950s with little practical knowledge thought that a boat driver should sit there, too. In some types of boats this is acceptable, but it is actually much more comfortable and safer for the driver to be located near the stern in a small, fast powerboat. The "front end" can be whipping up and down, with the seats right over the spot where the hull and water meet in successive poundings on each wave, while the after section is relatively stable and smooth riding. As designers became smarter and the showy but impractical boats began to disappear from the market, more and more builders began putting their control station near the stern along with the boat's primary seating.

In an all-purpose boat a convertible layout can greatly increase the boat's functions. By shifting a seat from athwartships for riding to fore and aft while at anchor, a cockpit can be made into a lounge or entertainment unit, or even a sleeping area. Backrests can be reversed to make seats face aft for fishing or water-skier watching, and in some boats a cockpit area can be cleared for use by swimmers or skin divers.

We have mentioned in the previous chapter that boats designed for a specific type of fishing have special layout and seating requirements, and these can vary as much as the types of fish being caught. In general, a good small open fishing boat should have a clear area for handling the rod or rods, free from obstructions and interference, and with the coaming and side decks in the fishing area free of cleats or other fittings that could snag lines. Stowage of rods and tackle and ready access to them for a quick change of equipment as the situation warrants are very important; there should also be a good place to keep the catch. Fishing-boat layout is a complete art in itself, and the newcomer should consult an expert on the 101 details that should be considered beyond these few generalities.

Stowage is important on any boat, and a system of lockers, drawers, and shelves utilizing all available space without being obtrusive is the tip-off to a well-thought-out boat. When good space engineering has been applied in this way, the odds are that the rest of the boat has been well designed, too. It is just as bad to try to put too much into a boat as it is to skimp on stowage, so a good balance is desirable. When looking at a new boat in the showroom, visualize her with several people, their life jackets, food, fishing tackle, swimming gear, and the boat's required equipment all on board, and then decide whether she has a good layout.

With some of the above provisions in mind, check off the functions you want a boat to perform and then decide whether she has the right specifications. How many people will normally be aboard? Will you do much fishing? Is water-skiing in the picture? Will you occasionally use her for overnight camping? Can she be trailed (almost all smallpower boats can be)? Can the seating arrangements and stowage facilities handle these requirements, or will you all be sitting just as though you were in the family car? Almost all boats are rated for their carrying capacity, indicated by a manufacturer's plate attached to the hull, and this should be checked and adhered to.

Power Plant

The outboard motor is by far the most popular power plant for small open powerboats and with good reason. It has been especially designed and refined for this usage for decades. It is now a sophisticated, reliable piece of equipment that performs a great many and varied functions and offers a wide range of power categories from 1½ horsepower up to 125 and more. It is not the only choice, however.

INBOARDS

Some small boats have inboard engines and there are a few cases in which this makes sense. In some kinds of fishing, the transom should be smooth and clear and an outboard would be in the way. There are hull types, especially long, narrow displacement hulls, in which placement of the weight aft is wrong. An inboard engine gives quicker, more positive control, especially in reverse, and a displacement hull for operations in rough water would be better off with an inboard. An outboard is least handy in heavy following seas, such as running inlets or a tide rip, when the shallow location of the propeller does not give much control surface. Where speed is not a consideration, continuous operation at low r.p.m.s is more comfortable with an inboard. At the other end of the scale, if you want the best in speed and power, an inboard engine can provide more, usually in the upper size range of open boats.

STERN DRIVES

These combine some advantages of both inboards and outboards. The power plant is inside the boat, the permanent part of it on an interior engine bed, while the propulsion unit is outside the transom. The major advantage of a stern drive is that it keeps the main section clear of machinery for greater versatility in arrangements and greater carrying capacity, while providing the power range of a regular inboard. In a broad-sterned, high-speed boat it is often better to have the weight of the power plant(s) in the extreme stern.

Stern drive on a deep-V hull

OUTBOARDS

Outboards run the gamut from peewee sewing machines of 1½ horsepower to monsters of 100 times that power and more. As the weight-to-power ratio has improved over the years with advanced technology in lightweight materials and gearing, more horsepower has been put into smaller packages so that increased power can be offered without increasing the size of the motor—too much machinery weight hanging off the transom of a boat is not good engineering.

The outboard motor has obvious advantages. Cost per horsepower and allowance for installation are both low compared with inboard or stern drive. Portability of all but the biggest models means ease of maintenance, security from theft, and flexibility. (Take a motor with you on vacation and just rent a boat when you get there.) Location of the power plants outside the boat adds to available space and reduces fire hazards. Service and fuel are generally available in all areas, and fuel can be easily obtained whatever the location of the boat because of the portability of the gas cans. Noise levels and reliability now match any other form of marine power.

There was a time when twin outboard installations were popular, but difficulties in synchronization and control and in building a transom to take them, plus the lighter weight of the top horsepower models, brought about a general return to single installations. Some owners do carry a small motor for trolling at low speeds and as a reserve in case the main engine quits.

As mentioned, one of the weaknesses of an outboard is boat control in a rough following sea, though modern hull types have helped to lessen this objection. Also, outboards do not reverse too well and they are not intended for long periods of operation at low speed, though this last characteristic has been improved some in recent years.

Outboard motors range in size from a few horsepower to 150 or more.

ROTARY ENGINES

As this is written, rotary cam engines in both outboard and inboard applications have not yet come on the market for the general public. They have been around for many years in experimental versions of the Wankel engine, and there is every likelihood that they will eventually be a factor in the regular marine market.

A general word about safety: every boat, no matter what the type of power plant, has a safe limit of horsepower, also indicated by a manufacturer's plate, and this should be followed strictly. Overloading and overpowering small boats are the two major causes of boating accidents, and it is imperative not to exceed these safety limits. A good dealer will not sell an overpowered boat, and he should also make sure the buyer understands the carrying capacity.

Equipment

Buying a boat, motor, and trailer is only the beginning. Then comes the equipment, and never forget this in your financial figuring. It can range from a relatively minimum outlay for a small open boat to almost double the base price in the case of an ocean-racing auxiliary.

There are two categories of equipment: what is legally required by the Coast Guard and/or state authorities and what is needed by the individual owner. The Coast Guard has classes of boats rated by length, with minimum requirements for each. The bulk of small open boats comes under Class A (less than 16 feet), while some may come under Class 1 (16 to 26 feet). You should check the full requirements each year, but briefly they are: for Class A, 1 backfire flame arrester on inboard engines, 2 ventilation ducts for inboards, 1 personal flotation device (PFD)— 1 of 3 types of life vests or a buoyant cushion—for every person on board, and a portable fire extinguisher. Class 1 adds to the same requirements a hand- or mouth-operated whistle audible at least half a mile.

Running lights required for both classes of powerboat are a combination red-and-green bow light of 20 points, visible 1 mile, and a 32-point white stern light visible 2 miles.

Not legally required but absolutely essential for operation are an anchor and line (I prefer a Danforth-type anchor for this size boat with nylon line; most dealers have a chart to relate anchor size and line diameter to boat size), mooring lines, fenders, first-aid kit, a bucket, pump or bailer, sponge, compass, boat hook, and perhaps a paddle. Other supplies depend on the owner's individual requirements, but here is a list of the most frequently needed items in a well-equipped small powerboat: radio (with weather station marked), flares, flashlight, knife, basic tools, charts of the local area, ice chest or cooler, binoculars, swimming ladder, can opener, ashtray, ice pick, engine spares, foul-weather gear, extra windbreakers, sunglasses, suntan lotion, eating utensils, navigation equipment as needed, flags, and burgees.

On some boats performance can be improved by the use of trim tabs, small flaps attached to the after end of the underbody and extending out from the transom. Their trim can be controlled and adjusted from the driving position to give the boat its best angle of attitude to the water. If the tabs are depressed, this will tend to lift the stern and keep the boat at a level attitude while planing, preventing the bow from rising too high. When her bow is riding high, a boat tends to bounce up and down as she hits the waves, and visibility is also impaired. Not all boats require trim tabs, but some designers specify them, not as a corrective measure but as a positive control over performance under different conditions.

7

❦♫♫♫♫♫♫♫♫♫♫♫♫♫♫♫♫♫♫♫♫♫♫♫❦

Small Sailboats for Daysailing

In sailboats the counterpart of the small open powerboat is the daysailer. As defined previously, this is a small open sailboat not intended for racing. Just as the outboard runabout is the most popular form of small powerboat, the daysailer is the single most popular sailboat. A daysailer may have a small outboard for auxiliary power when the wind quits or the tide or current is in the wrong direction. The motor is literally an auxiliary, however, and the boat is intended primarily for sailing.

In this field, also, there are as many choices of boats as there are manufacturers, all of whom have brand names for their products. Some daysailers are distributed nationally by big companies through dealers while others are mainly localized, confined to an area near the builder, who sells directly to the public. The brand names can be confusing, but the choice of basic types is not too complicated.

Boardboats

To start with, there are the boardboats, the surfboardlike craft between 12 and 15 feet with one simple sail, that are really a bathing-suit operation for one or two people. The Sailfish, and then the Sunfish, brand names for Alcort, Inc., popularized this breed soon after World War II. First they were simple hollow plywood boards and many of them were built from kits, but fiberglass took over by the 1960s. There are many competitive brands, though the Sunfish is still the single most popular and widely sold sailboat in history.

There are a few things to remember about boardboats. First, they are wonderful basic trainers. If the sun is warm and the wind isn't too strong, almost anyone can climb aboard and pick up a few rudiments. Since you get wet while sailing one anyway, that gut fear of capsizing is not so strong and mistakes don't seem horrendous. A novice, once he figures where the wind is from, can make a boardboat behave to some extent and gain confidence in the process. After one sail on a boardboat, you won't have learned all there is to know about handling a boat under sail, but some of the mystery will have been dispelled. If you do capsize, it's a simple thing to push down on the dagger board, right the boat, and give it another go.

Novices should take care, however, not to operate a boardboat when there is a strong offshore wind on an open body of water. Since windward work is harder to grasp than reaching and running, there is the danger of a novice being blown offshore and unable to fight back. Beware also of cold water which can reduce physical effectiveness suddenly and rapidly, thus making a capsize a much more serious affair.

In rough water boardboats are difficult to handle without considerable experience. They will surf beautifully downwind but need constant control. And they do not go windward well in really rough seas. As a "people's sailboat," however, they are unbeatable.

Dinghies

Some daysailers are even smaller than the boardboats, but they can give an impression of being more of a boat because they have real hulls as opposed to a flat board shape with a foot well. Prams and dinghies as small as 7½ feet can be sailed by adults, or more comfortably by children, in protected waters and are great for poking about bays, creeks, ponds, and rivers as long as caution is used about venturing into open waters where a sudden rough sea might kick up. As cartoppers, or shoved into the back of a station wagon, little sailing dinghies of this type can provide a great deal of fun. Many owners of large cruising yachts equip their tender as a sailing dinghy for quiet drifting around an anchorage at the end of a day's passage. There was one period in our family career when the only yacht we owned was an 8-foot sailing pram, and we had many delightful adventures in her. Even when the two older kids were 4 and 2, it was a bit crowded with the whole family aboard, but we managed some fascinating expeditions, usually in shifts.

Progressing to slightly larger boats, you come to another one of those basic decisions, and this one is keel versus centerboard. This is largely decided by geography. If you are in an area of shallow water, flats, and sandbars, you should have a centerboarder. If you operate off somewhere like Maine, or almost the entire Pacific Coast where you are either on shore or in deep water, there is no need to put up with a centerboarder's inherent weaknesses.

Centerboarders

The basic advantage of a centerboard is ability to operate in shoal water. The typical centerboarder has a relatively flat, shoal-draft hull of perhaps a foot or two that will not

DAYSAILERS:
boardboat, dingy (sail
#53) and small one-
design centerboard
sloop (Flying Junior),
centerboard sloop
(Snipe); (*facing page*)
18-foot keel sloop
(Typhoon), swing keel
sloop, 16-foot sloop
with outboard
auxiliary

proceed to windward unless it has some means of preventing it from slipping sideways. A sailboat needs some sort of underwater lateral resistance to convert the pressure of the wind on the sails from a sideways direction, which tends to tip the boat over and push it directly away from the wind, into a forward thrust. Some sort of deep fin provides this resistance. If it is fixed in place, it is a keel. If it can be lowered when needed and raised when not, it is called a centerboard (and sometimes a swing keel). A centerboard is controlled by a rope or wire called a pennant and can be adjusted at various depths. When raised all the way, it fits into a narrow vertical housing on the centerline of the boat called a centerboard trunk. When a centerboarder is sailing across the wind or before it, the board is not needed and the boat can operate in very shallow water. If it is necessary to go to windward in shallow water, the depth of the board can be adjusted. It is not as efficient at partial depths as when all the way down, or nearly so, but it will work. Daggerboards (boards raised and lowered vertically) are a variation on the type.

For beaching a boat or putting her on a trailer, the board can be pulled up into the trunk where it is completely out of the way. Most centerboard boats also have a shallow rudder, or one that tips up if it hits an obstruction, so that the depth of the hull is the controlling draft.

A centerboard has inherent disadvantages. The centerboard trunk requires a slot through the keel, the timber or member that is the boat's central element, and this tends to weaken the construction. It was more of a problem in the days of wooden boats because leaks around the centerboard trunk were a traditional problem. Now that fiberglass has taken over, the problem of leaks and weakness isn't as pronounced, but it is still there.

It is also more difficult to shape a centerboard in the most efficient way for top performance, and the skipper must learn the best depth and angle to set the board for the best balance. A centerboard boat is lighter, without outside ballast (ballast is weight added to a boat to increase stability, and outside ballast means that it is attached to the keel permanently and is very efficient). A centerboarder is therefore more tender and more easily capsized than a keelboat. A centerboard trunk also takes up extra room in the cockpit of a boat, breaking it up and making movement awkward. There are factors to be weighed against the flexibility provided by shallow-water operation. Where we are, on the Shrewsbury River which has an overall depth of about 2½ feet at low tide, there is no choice. It's a centerboarder or stay home at low tide.

Since a centerboarder is more sensitive, due to the need for adjusting the depth of the board and due to the lighter weight of the whole boat, it is actually more of a challenge and can teach a novice more about the forces of wind on a boat in a shorter time than a keelboat. It used to be said on Barnegat Bay in New Jersey that anyone who learned to sail in the shallow, light, over-rigged centerboarders known as Barnegat Sneakboxes had learned all the tricks a sailboat can pull.

And still the basic choice is one of geography.

Keelboats

In a daysailer, if you don't need a centerboard, the room gained in the cockpit is itself enough of a determining factor. A keelboat is considered safer because it is harder to capsize, although a keelboat that heels far enough over to be swamped may not have positive buoyancy because of the weight on her keel and could sink. Positive buoyancy in the form of flotation tanks or some type of foam is an important safety factor in a keelboat.

While not as skittishly sensitive as a centerboarder, a keelboat can be wonderfully responsive and have a real "feel" as she accommodates to the water. A well-designed keelboat is also a better bet to be a good sea boat in rough going. If your daysailing takes you into potentially rough, open waters, a keelboat should give you a better sense of security.

Swing-Keel Boats

A keelboat is more difficult to trail, and should this be in your plans, it would be better to have a centerboarder or a swing-keel boat. The swing keel was developed mainly on the West Coast, where there is no need for a centerboarder while afloat. All of the harbors open onto deep water, but there are so few facilities that there was need for a type of boat that could be stored at home and trailed to different launching areas. For this, the swing keel was developed. This simply means a keel that is fixed in place all the time while sailing but can be unbolted and slipped up into a trunk or slot while the boat is being trailed. A swing keel is ballasted and therefore more difficult to operate than is a centerboard while under way. A strong tackle or even a hydraulic pump is provided for raising and lowering a swing keel.

Hull Forms

Sailboats have the same basic division between V-bottom and round-bottom that was discussed in the last chapter about small powerboats, but there are not as many variations in the two types. There are catamarans (twin-hulled boats) as small daysailers; there are some with modified catamaran or tunnel underbodies; and a few people sail small trimarans, though this hull form is not well suited to daysailers.

The V-bottom form is well suited to shallow draft and is quite often found in centerboarders, but the basic reason for a V-bottomed sailboat has largely become obsolete. In the days of wooden construction, this was the cheapest and easiest form to put together, often in sheet plywood and often by home builders, hence its popularity. In fiberglass and aluminum there is no real reason to have a hard-chine boat unless one needs a very shallow draft for special circumstances. Hard-chine construction does not actually lend itself as well to molded construction and has been carried on only because of the longevity of certain classes of boats that, while converted to fiberglass construction, date back to the days of wood.

Round-bottom construction can lend itself to a centerboard or a keel configuration, and in these days of fiberglass molding can be accomplished with sophisticated shapes that were impossible in wood. Our Sanderling catboat, for example, benefited from modern materials. Her bow sections were hollowed out and made much finer in molded construction because the aluminum mast was so much lighter than the old-fashioned "telephone poles" of the wooden boat's day. The hull did not have to provide so much weight support and could be formed in a better configuration for sailing performance.

For planing sailboats a flat bottom with rounded bilges makes a very efficient hull, but most daysailing owners are probably not looking so much for planing performance as for comfort and seaworthiness. A round-bottomed hull should be fairly dry and seaworthy with an easy motion in a chop or sea. For a comfortable daysailer, the best hull shape would be one with good beam, fairly hard bilges for stability, and a modified "hour-glass" underbody for comfort.

Layouts and Accommodations

The cockpit is extremely important in a daysailer. It should have good wide seats with comfortable backrests and a place to brace your feet when the boat is tipping.

There should be plenty of stowage space under the seats and under the side decks, and a popular addition on many daysailers is a small cuddy cabin forward for stowing gear. If children are aboard it can be a great place for "playing house" or just taking a nap, as well as a shelter for little ones against sudden bad weather. In some boats it might even be big enough for some overnight camping with air mattresses and sleeping bags. It is also possible to buy or contrive some form of cockpit tent for a daysailer that rigs over the boom and makes a snugly protected sleeping place out of the cockpit seats or floorboards. If a cockpit does not have seats, by the way, and you are expected to spend all your time on the floorboards, the sailing will not be very comfortable for any length of time.

Beware of a boat that has too much crammed into too little space. I once saw a 17-foot sloop at a boat show that actually had a small cabin forward and a small cabin aft of the cockpit. She was a European import and Europeans may be smaller or mind discomfort less, but most Americans wouldn't put their dogs in these cabins, and the cockpit was also cramped. Comfortable daysailers can range from about 13 feet up close to 30, when they become something of an extravagance. The ideal size is about 18 feet.

Rigs

There are really only two basic rigs that make sense in a daysailer: catboat and sloop. The boardboats are often rigged with a lateen sail, a single sail on a gaff and boom that meet in a V at the forward end of the sail. They, instead of the sail, are attached to the mast, and the whole thing can be raised and dropped very simply. It's a fine rig for such a small boat but less efficient in bigger sizes.

A catboat rig is simply one sail on a mast stepped right

in the bow. As pointed out in Chapter 5, some catboats can have a ketch or yawl rig, but this is very rare, especially in small boats. The catboat is one place where you will still find the gaff rig used rather regularly. Because the mast is stepped so far forward in a catboat, it is difficult to brace it with side stays. The deck is so narrow at the base of the mast that there is no real spread to the stays, and the angle is too sharp for them to lend good support. Only a short mast will stand without stays. Therefore, to get a taller sail on a short mast, the gaff rig is used. The gaff is a spar on the top of the sail that is raised at a sharp V angle to the mast so that it extends the top of the sail far above the top of the mast and allows more sail area than a simple Marconi rig (a triangular sail that ends at the top of the mast) could provide.

The gaff rig requires more sweat to raise because of the two halyards, and it can be a big, ungainly expanse to get down in a blow, but it is still an efficient sail. A built-in safety factor is "scandalizing the peak." This old sailors' term merely means dropping the gaff quickly, which effectively cuts the sail area almost in half in a matter of seconds—a handy quality when a sudden squall hits.

There are catboats with Marconi rigs, but the taller mast just doesn't seem right and the sail is no more efficient. Our Sanderling is gaff-rigged and she will hold her own in sailing ability against any boat her size and weight. As for weight aloft, the weight of the gaff isn't appreciably more than that of a taller mast and stays. In cat-rigged dinghies there is not much need for a gaff because the rig can be lighter and a mast tall enough to hold a Marconi sail can be made strong enough with a minimum of staying. Here the extra weight and windage of a gaff would not be a good idea.

For most daysailers, however, a simple sloop rig is the answer. It is an easily handled, efficient rig, and the jib adds interest and some performance advantage (which seems to increase with the size of the boat). Although racing boats often carry a large overlapping jib, known as a "genoa" because it first made its appearance in a race in that Italian port in the 1920s, a simple working jib that just fills the foretriangle between the mast and the jibstay makes a lot more sense. It is much easier to tack and trim. For real lazy sailing a self-trimming jib on a club, or boom, can be rigged, and it only has to be tended when its trim is to be changed. A daysailer should be moderately under-rigged rather than carry a big spread of sail. There is no sense in making sailing into too much work if you're not racing. Roller-reefing gear or a set of reef points for reducing the size of the mainsail is a good idea if you expect much heavy wind where you operate.

For those who want real action while they sail, even if they're not racing, a spinnaker could be carried, but this big, colorful balloon of a sail is really a racing tool and requires skillful handling and trimming. It does enliven sailing greatly, but it is somewhat contrary to the spirit of daysailing. And full spinnaker gear adds considerably to the expense of a boat.

Auxiliary Power

Although there may be no need for help from a motor in some daysailers, depending on their location, and a good paddle may be enough to ensure your getting back to home base if the wind quits, the scope, mobility, and reliability of daysailers are greatly increased by the use of a small outboard motor for an auxiliary. I say outboard because most daysailers are too small to have space for an inboard, especially if they are centerboarders, and an inboard doesn't take as kindly to the infrequent use it gets in a small sailboat as does an outboard. Our first two daysailers had inboards back in the days when outboards were not as reliable or as well developed in operational features, but neither worked out too well.

For a sailboat up to 20 feet or so, a 3- or 5-horsepower motor is plenty and usually the smaller one is better unless you expect very strong currents where you operate. The smaller and lighter the motor, the easier it is to handle and to stow. It should be used on a bracket, not in a well, except in cases of special design. A well takes too much space away from a boat this size, and it presents problems in ventilation and in water slopping up through the aperture. We have a 7-horse motor on the Sanderling, a heavy boat for 18 feet, and it is more than enough. We have strong currents to contend with but could do with a 5 horse. We never had more than 7.5 on *Mar Claro,* and in fact, she operated well with a 6 horse most of the time. Make sure you have a long-shaft motor for sailboat use. In some cases it is possible to equip the motor with a special propeller for slow-speed operation.

Trailers

Trailers greatly expand daysailing activity. If a boat is being bought new from a dealer, he probably carries a trailer suited for the type boat. In general, don't skimp on specifications and make sure the car is properly set up, too.

For smaller boats the trailer should be capable of beach launching. It should be waterproofed against immersion with noncorrosive parts, sealed lights, etc. Larger boats are usually carried in a separate cradle fastened on a flat-bed trailer and must be handled for launching by an overhead movable lift in a boatyard rather than by immersing the trailer. There are so many variables in trailers that the only practical advice is to work with a yard or dealer who knows what type is suitable for the boat in question. This advice also applies to the decision on whether to have a trailer with brakes and whether to beef up the brakes of the tow car.

Equipment

Daysailers under 16 feet come under Class A in the Coast Guard equipment requirements, and from 16 to 26 feet they are in Class 1. Unless they have inboard engines, in which case they need a backfire flame arrester and ventilation ducts, Class A daysailers are only required to have a buoyant cushion or approved life vest for everyone on board, and Class 1 daysailers, an approved vest for everyone and one throwable device, plus a fire extinguisher if they have an outboard. Class 1 must also have a hand- or mouth-operated whistle. Running lights for both classes include a 20-point combination red-and-green bow light, visible 1 mile, and a 12-point white light in the stern. Under power the stern light must be 32 points in both classes, and in all cases, visible 2 miles.

These are the only legal requirements, but no one should operate a boat without an anchor and line (as in small powerboats, I prefer the Danforth with nylon line; consult your dealer for recommended anchor and rope sizes), mooring lines, fenders, first-aid kit, bucket, pump or bailer, sponge, compass, boat hook, paddle, and rigging spares.

A chart of local waters is almost always a necessity and according to your method of operations here are some other items usually needed on a well-equipped boat: radio (with weather station marked), flares, flashlight, knife with marlinespike, basic tools, ice chest or cooler, binoculars, swimming ladder, can opener, ashtray, ice pick, foul-weather gear, windbreakers, sunglasses, suntan lotion, eating utensils, navigation equipment as needed, flags and burgees, tide and current tables (in waters where they apply).

8

⟿⟿⟿⟿⟿⟿⟿⟿⟿⟿⟿⟿⟿⟿⟿⟿⟿⟿⟿⟿⟿⟿⟿⟿

Cabin Cruisers

By previous definition we have seen that a cabin cruiser is a motorboat with living accommodations, usually inboard powered. If outboard powered, a cabin boat is almost always referred to as an outboard cruiser. This latter type had a strong vogue in the 1950s but, except for very small boats with minimum accommodations, the recent trend has been to inboard power, and fiberglass is almost the universal construction material. Aluminum is used in a few cases, especially in larger boats; there is a minuscule ferrocement market, and a few custom builders in odd corners carry on in wood, but these are all exceptions to the general rule of using fiberglass.

Variations in accommodations create several subtypes: flying-bridge cruiser, trunk cabin cruiser, flush-deck cruiser, tri-cabin cruiser, motor yacht, trawler, sport fisherman, and, for want of a better category for the type, houseboat.

Except for houseboats, whose hull characteristics are quite different from the regular types of cruiser, there is less variation in hull form than applies to small open powerboats. It would be folly to build a flat-bottomed cruiser in anything but a houseboat configuration, and it is rare to see a cathedral or slot hull in anything but a small overnighter. The basic choice is between displacement hulls and planing hulls, and between V-bottom and round-bottom. In general, the V types are planing boats and the round-bottomed ones are displacement, but this is not a hard-and-fast rule. There is some crossover both ways.

The other major choice is in type of power, and this boils down to diesel or gasoline, to inboard or stern drive, and in inboard to the type of installation and gearing, direct or V drive.

Hull Forms

Most cruiser owners want to "have their cake and eat it too," which explains why planing boats are the most popular. The fact that it is expensive to achieve planing performance in a boat loaded with living accommodations has not deterred most owners from this requirement. Usually this means some form of V-bottomed hull, though not always.

V-BOTTOM

A traditional cruiser hull form has developed out of this requirement, and a version of it is included in the model line of just about every stock manufacturer. For ease of entry into waves, it features a moderately deep-V section forward which gradually lessens in dead rise (the angle of the transverse hull lines between the keel and the edges of the hull, or chines) toward the stern. From amidships to the stern, the dead rise lessens to a virtually flat area at the transom to give the lift necessary for planing performance. This is a relatively easy form to design and build, and its wide acceptance is testimony to the fact it does the job most people require of it. It is generally called a modified V and is seen more often than a V hull with constant dead rise.

Facing page: modern 24-foot cabin cruiser

There are variations in the amount of V, in the change in dead rise toward the stern, in the location of spray rails, and in the treatment of the chine area, but these are minor. Under most conditions and circumstances encountered by the average cruiser, this type of hull performs well and is an acceptable compromise. It is not prohibitively expensive to power onto a plane and achieve good speed. The ride is moderately comfortable, and the type is adequately seaworthy. All these qualifiers do mean, however, that there is compromise involved, and someone looking for ultimate performance in any one of these areas will have to seek something different.

Speed is mainly a question of power once a boat can be made to plane, and the more power available the faster the boat will go—at a price. In the V-bottom type, it is not only not cheap but means a rough, pounding ride if the sea is up, so that there are many times when it is impossible to make use of a boat's speed potential without

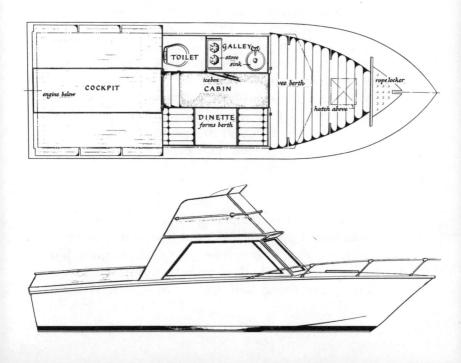

shaking the passengers' teeth loose. At slower speeds the hull is not too efficient and creates drag.

Another disdavantage of the V-bottom type with a broad flat stern, as discussed under small powerboats, is the difficulty of steering in a following sea, especially in inlets or tide rips. An inboard boat with bigger rudders than the small control surfaces an outboard has underwater does steer better, but it is still difficult to keep this type from broaching when a sea gets under the broad flat stern and the chine digs in as the boat corkscrews to one side, accentuating the twisting motion.

Since a V-bottomed hull usually has good beam, it provides good space for accommodations. Initial stability is also good, but the motion in a steep cross sea can be jerky and uncomfortable.

All these are items to consider in choosing a hull. The all-around compromise of the typical modified V-bottomed cruiser hull is a good one for the use that most of the boats are put to, and it is justifiably a popular type because of these compromises. Unless you plan a considerable amount of high-speed offshore work, and if you are willing to pay the price in initial engine installation costs and continuing fuel costs for the speed obtainable, it is a logical choice for a cruiser hull.

The V-bottom type made special sense in the days of wooden construction, as it was easier and cheaper to put together. The hard chine, when properly handled in the design, also serves as a good spray deflector, and as noted, initial stability is good.

ROUND-BOTTOM

The round-bottom or round-bilge type has usually been associated with a deep, displacement-type hull, gaining in seaworthiness what it gives away in speed potential, but it isn't quite that simple. It is perfectly possible to have a fast, high-performance hull with a basic round-bottom shape. Many of the best sport fishermen used to have this shape, but the trend has been to the modified V because of better stability at low speeds for trolling offshore.

A hull with rounded bilges can still be flattened out in the after section of the underbody for planing performance while retaining a rounded entry to cut down on the tendency to pound.

Much more frequently, however, round-bottomed hulls will be found in the offshore cruisers known as trawler types with displacement hulls, low speed potential, and good seakeeping ability. Though round-bottomed hulls have a tendency to roll in a cross sea, this is reduced by the depth and displacement of the hull, and the motion is still easier and smoother than in a V-bottom which tends to roll jerkily because of the action of waves under the chines. A round-bottomed hull can also be more efficient, with less drag, for displacement operation. There are displacement V hulls in use, but usually with a loss of engine efficiency, as compared to a round-bottomed hull.

DEEP-V

The deep-V was originally developed for small boats, but it has been adapted to much bigger hulls, and luxury yachts up in the 60-foot range are being built to this configuration. As in small powerboats, the advantages are a nonpounding ride at good speeds in rough water and good directional stability. Seakeeping qualities are excellent under all conditions. In the deep-V, pronounced dead rise is carried all the way aft, and longitudinal stringers help with directional stability, lift, and spray deflection.

Again, the main disadvantage is the high cost of the power needed to get this type on top and keep it there. Engines must be on the large side and use quantities of fuel, which means that extra space must be devoted to the power plants and to tankage, cutting down on room for accommodations. Also, this hull form has poor initial stability at low speeds, and the motion while trolling in a cross sea or a confused sea can be unpredictable and a bit jumpy.

If you do want speed in a boat and you want to have it under all conditions without being forced to throttle back when the sea kicks up, the deep-V is really the answer. The ride qualities are markedly better than in the other types.

CATAMARANS

There has been a limited use of catamaran hulls for powerboats. With a big platform placed across two small, easily driven hulls, the type lends itself particularly well to party-fishing boat use, where large groups are to be carried on deck with no need for much in the way of interior accommodations. These of necessity must be cut up and minimal, compared to the same length of monohull. Also, while the catamaran offers an extremely stable ride in moderate conditions, it lacks ultimate stability for really rough cross seas.

Layouts and Accommodations

A cabin cruiser is intended for living aboard, and the way this is done has infinite variations. The most important thing to look for in accommodations is the manner in which space is used. Is the amount of space available used sensibly, or is too much crammed into it in an attempt to provide more than should reasonably be expected? The 22-foot outboard cruiser we had in our family was a perfect example of the latter. She was a "four-sleeper" by the builder's definition, and this was fine for our family at the time—we intended no long cruises and the kids enjoyed sleeping aboard as a lark. For serious cruising, however, she was totally inadequate. The bunks were for children or midgets, the head was enclosed but had all the room of a tight-fitting coffin, and there wasn't an inch of stowage space anywhere. You had to sleep with your toothbrush to bring one aboard. This oversupply of inadequate accommodations also cut down on the cockpit space and made the cabin trunk and hull so high that the boat didn't handle well in any kind of wind. She had too much surface and windage.

If she had been an inboard with the engine box in the middle of the cockpit, she would have been even more cramped, although she might not have been so difficult to control.

Many lessons have been learned since those midfifties' days, and there aren't as many evidences of the tendency to overdo the accommodations. A 22-footer should be comfortable for two, and a snug, well-planned cabin can be provided in this length. For a young family who can afford only this size boat and who still want to take the children along overnight, or occasionally another couple, air mattresses in the cockpit with a tent over it would make more sense. This occasional makeshift is better than permanently ruining the boat's fixed accommodations.

Be careful of other layout aberrations. We were once loaned a cabin cruiser for a week which was a comfortable, well-planned boat except that the enclosed head, which had fine privacy on the cabin side, had a large "picture window" that gave right into the cockpit. If people were in the cockpit, the only way to avoid that goldfish-bowl feeling was to have someone stand with his back to the window. Sometimes a drawer will be placed where it can't be opened fully, or a ladder where it can't be moved without scraping knuckles. It's amazing how little things like this can sour your attitude about a whole boat that might otherwise be well designed and well planned.

Check the cabin out for hanging lockers, shelf space, tool drawers, area for working on charts, position of lights, ease of working in the galley, communication between the galley and the cockpit. If these things have been planned with ingenuity and common sense, the whole boat is probably well designed. If it is a jackass layout, the whole boat may be a lemon.

TRUNK CABIN CRUISER

For years this has been the most popular and most conventional layout for a moderate-sized boat. There is an open cockpit aft, sometimes with a top all the way aft, though more often with a partial top extending from a windshield back over the control station at the forward end of the cockpit. The cabin, reached through a doorway from the cockpit on the opposite side from the helmsman's seat, will be a step or two down, and, depending on the

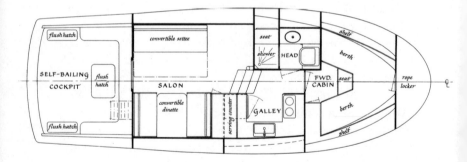

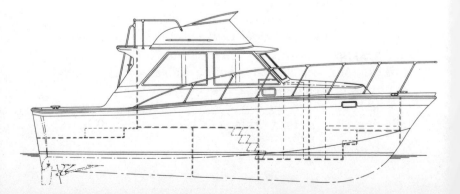

size of the boat, there will be two or four bunks, a head, and galley space. These of course can be moved around in endlessly varied combinations. The cabin is enclosed by a trunk rising above the deck and set in from the side of the boat to give passageway fore and aft on the side decks. Many boats include a dinette that can be converted to a double bunk at night as part of the main cabin layout with a galley opposite, a separate cabin with 2 V berths forward, and an enclosed head in between.

If a boat is under 25 feet, the layout would have to be particularly ingenious and well thought out, and the hull would have to be very roomy for the length, perhaps sacrificing seaworthiness, to make more than a 2-berth layout workable. You will see many "four-sleepers" advertised under this size but check out how they really work for four people.

The trunk-cabin layout is popular up into the 35-foot range. It is an excellent all-purpose layout because the open cockpit aft is good for fishing, swimming, or, if there is sufficient speed, towing and watching water-skiers; there is some shelter from sun or weather, and the cabin can be arranged in a comfortable way. In most boats the greater part of time on board is spent in the cockpit, and it makes sense to have this a roomy, comfortable area. If your need is for maximum accommodations, one of the layouts discussed below might be more suitable.

Flying-bridge cruiser

By building a permanent, strong structure over the forward end of the cockpit, a second control station can be placed above it. Usually this means two sets of controls, with the one in the main cockpit serving in bad weather. The flying bridge gives the helmsman much greater visibility all around the boat. This is a great safety factor under way, almost a must for serious fishing, and also a

Facing page: 34-foot trunk cabin cruiser

32-foot aluminum flying-bridge cruiser

big help in docking the boat. Aside from practicalities, the aesthetics of being up there are pleasant (though my aesthetic sense is offended when it is referred to as a "flybridge").

A flying bridge can be placed on almost any kind of layout, though it is naturally most popular on boats with an open after cockpit that is suitable for fishing.

A flying bridge adds to the cost of a boat, and it also adds topside weight. If for any reason the boat has a critical stability problem, the addition of a flying bridge might be too much, but this would be rare under modern conditions.

FLUSH-DECK CRUISER

In this style the accommodations are all under the deck, which is then an unbroken line from bow to stern or, on what is called a raised-deck layout, from the bow to a break at the cockpit. If there is enough height in the hull to make a flush deck possible, it naturally provides more deck space. In bigger boats a deckhouse, a cabin built right on top of the main deck rather than through it like a trunk cabin, can provide a great deal of extra space. It is not unusual to have all the sleeping accommodations below, with the deckhouse used for a control station and lounge or dining area, or combination of both. It is difficult to come up with a flush-deck and deckhouse arrangement in boats under 35 feet, though attempts have been made. One way that this can be done is in a displacement hull with a low flush deck, a deep hull, and a tugboatlike deckhouse. Much smaller boats can have a practical arrangement of this sort, but it is harder to achieve in the V-hull planing-type boat.

TRI-CABIN CRUISER

This is a boat with an extra cabin in the stern. Sometimes it is a small trunk cabin that merely cuts off the after end of the cockpit. More often it is seen in a flush-deck hull. Once you use the stern of the boat for accommodations, you have reduced its adaptability for fishing and for ease of swimming and water-skiing. There has been a tendency to put this layout in boats of shorter and shorter overall length, creating very high freeboard and a bulky-looking boat that seems to have been chopped in two and the after end disposed of somewhere else. Since the stern of the boat is usually the widest part, therefore the roomiest, it does increase accommodation space for people who don't worry about the other functions.

MOTOR YACHT

As pointed out in the definitions in Chapter 5, this is a flexible term that depends on the owner and/or manufacturer. Usually it means something over 45 feet with elaborate accommodations and a lounge and entertainment area completely separated from the sleeping quarters. Stock motor yachts are available up to close to 70 feet. From there up most of the boats are custom built, or

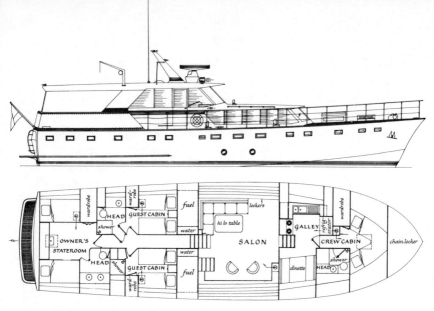

66-foot modern yacht

at least custom fitted on a standard hull. There are very few yachts over 100 feet being built or operated in the United States anymore. To see a collection of them, go to the Riviera or to the plusher harbors in Greece.

TRAWLER

This has become an increasingly popular type as more and more people retire afloat and make their boat their permanent home. To them time is not important. They don't have to get 50 miles offshore to the fishing grounds and back in one day, and they don't have to make hundreds of miles over a weekend, or New York to Florida in six days. They want comfort, low maintenance, and economy of operation in a reliable boat that will see them through the inevitable rough spots.

The trawler type, or offshore cruiser, can range from a tugboatlike craft under 30 feet to a major yacht of twice that size. Most trawlers are flush deck with a deckhouse, and an open deck area aft that serves in place of a cockpit. The deckhouse roof can also be used as deck space. Some have a small steadying sail, but it is not used for propulsion. Almost all have diesel power, with single screw predominating. A frequent backup measure is to set up the generator so it can be hooked to the main drive shaft and propel the boat at slow speed in case of complete failure of the main engine.

Trawler types seldom make more than about 9 knots, and there is a compromise somewhere if they go faster. This means economy of operation, especially with diesel. They can maintain this kind of speed through conditions that would slow a conventional planing boat down to the same or even lower speed.

You have to know exactly what you are and are not getting when you settle for a trawler, but those who want her characteristics swear by the type.

Sport fisherman

We have already seen that there are almost as many kinds of fishing boats as there are kinds of fish, but the basic thing to remember about any sport fisherman is that she is a machine for catching fish and nothing else. Those who

34-foot trawler

fish casually and also cruise on their boats have, in effect, a platform for catching fish, but not a machine. On a true sport fisherman the cockpit (the nerve center of the boat), the power plant(s), the controls, and the accommodations are only there in relation to the function of fishing. Nothing in the way of extra gear or accommodations should compromise this function.

In general, the term sport fisherman applies to a boat from 25 to 50 feet which is able to go out in rough water at good speed (and therefore usually a modified-V or deep-V hull) with a good range to go far offshore, troll all day, and still make it back the same night. The cockpit and fishing chairs must be arranged so that there is no interference with playing the lines when a fish is hooked and with landing it when it is beaten. There must be a good area to keep the fish that are brought aboard, plus bait, and good stowage for all the rods and tackle that are needed. Although some of the larger boats are set up for limited cruising comfort and a few big custom jobs have luxury cabins forward of the fishing area, most true sport fishermen only have a day galley and a couple of bunks for whatever crew lives aboard or ferries her from area to area.

HOUSEBOAT

The development of self-propelled houseboats was a phenomenon of the early sixties that has leveled off considerably. A houseboat has house-trailerlike accommodations on a flat, flush-decked hull that is really a barge or a scow with perhaps a shallow V underbody. Some houseboat types are placed in hulls with a cruiser-type bow, intended for moderately rough water, but the most popular type is for inland waters. Propulsion can be by outboard, stern drive, or inboard V drive, depending on the size of the boat. Houseboats provide by far the most space for overall length of any kind of cabin craft, but they are only intended for sheltered waters. They might venture outside on a calm day but should never go so far that they could get caught in a weather change offshore. They should be considered a house first and a boat second, for safety's sake.

Power

Power for the cabin cruiser boils down to that basic gas versus diesel choice and then to a question of method of installation. The pluses for gasoline power are lower initial cost; wider range of selection in sizes, horsepower, and price; availability of fuel; and wider familiarity with the type for servicing. Weight per horsepower is another advantage of gasoline, though advances in this respect have been made in the diesel field. Some people also do not like the diesel smell that is ever present.

The two big advantages of diesel are safety and economy of operation. A diesel engine is much safer in that gasoline is a more volatile fuel and the danger of explosion is always present if the fuel is mishandled in any way. Diesel fuel is also a great deal cheaper, though the engine must be run for a good many hours before the lower cost of fuel makes up for the initial higher cost of the engine. Diesel engines generally have the reputation of not being quite as temperamental as gas engines, especially in boats where an engine may lay idle for days at a time between periods of use.

Where to put the engine is a matter of the boat's design. Stern drives clear the main living area of machinery, but they take away cockpit space. If the boat's design calls for engine weight in the stern, a V-drive installation may be the answer, again keeping the main section of the boat clear while still allowing for a true inboard engine. In larger boats it may be possible to keep the entire installation under the cockpit sole and not reduce cockpit space either.

On the subject of single versus twin screw, there is no denying that twin screw gives greater reliability, maneuverability, and speed. It is mainly a question of whether you want to pay the rather heavy price of a twin installation to get these advantages. For offshore work twin screw is almost a must, as no one wants to be stranded miles from home with an inoperative power plant. Twin screw is a blessing in docking and maneuvering, and in getting those extra knots. You just have to decide whether you want to pay the installation and fuel bills.

Equipment

When we got into the cruiser range, we are talking about much more sophisticated equipment than is needed in small open powerboats and sailboats. First of all, there are more legal requirements over 26 feet than for boats in Classes A and 1. From 26 to 40 feet is Class 2, and 40 to 65 is Class 3. A fog bell is an added requirement (only to be rung while anchored in a fog), the whistle must be audible 1 mile, and the fire extinguisher requirements are more stringent. Running lights call for 2 1-mile, 10-point sidelights, red to port, green to starboard; a 20-point white bow light visible 2 miles; and a 32-point, 2-mile stern light. Light regulations are slightly different in International Rules, and on the Great Lakes in some cases, and should be checked upon taking over a boat.

No dealer is going to let a boat go out without the correct safety equipment required for her class, and the rest of the basic needs should be aboard every boat, too: anchor, chain and line, fenders, mooring lines, first-aid kit, and boat hook.

From here on, the list can get as long as your arm, depending on the size and type of boat, the amount of time to be spent aboard, and your involvement with electronics. Just a minimum list includes compass, radio, flares, flashlights and spotlight, tool kit, spare parts, binoculars, charts and navigation equipment, swimming ladder, galley gear, ashtrays, foul-weather gear and spare windbreakers, sunglasses, flags and burgees, tide and current tables, dinghy (perhaps with an outboard motor), swabs and sponges, bedding, towels, extra cushions. This can be expanded with almost any item found in a well-equipped house or apartment if you plan to set up real housekeeping on the boat.

In electronics two of the most important items are a depth sounder and two-way radio. Current regulations on radio-aboard-pleasure-craft should be checked, with VHF as the minimum requirement. A radio direction finder is another vital item. The full range of electronic gear can make a boat's bridge look like the cockpit of an airliner, and all of it has a place on the complete, well-operated boat. One thing to remember is that the more gear a boat has on board, the more there is that will need servicing and maintenance and be likely to break down. Think over each item carefully and decide whether you really need it. And none of it is cheap. Nothing runs the cost of a boat up more quickly than a full range of electronic equipment.

If the boat is to have a load of electronics, she should have a generator if possible, and of course, a shore-connection rig to take electricity from the land when tied up. As for the items to consider, they run like this: radar, loran, shore-current adapter, bilge sniffer (to detect fumes in the bilge), various alarms for engine malfunction, air-conditioning, mechanical refrigeration, hot water, pressurized water, engine synchronization instrumentation, and various forms of navigation gear like ADF and Omni. Again, analyze carefully what you really need.

9

Cruising Auxiliaries

Not too long ago, one chapter could have covered both cruising auxiliaries and offshore racers as the breeds were practically one and the same. Almost every ocean-racing boat was expected to be used for cruising on occasion and roomy, comfortable cruising boats were not out of place in an occasional turn in the Bermuda Race or Transpac, or some shorter coastal competition.

Gradually, however, the pressures of competition brought refinements to offshore racing boats that were incompatible with cruising comfort, both in hull design and in accommodations and layout. By the early 1970s when the International Offshore Rules came into general use for major offshore events, the split had become so pronounced that a whole new category of pure cruising boats soon came into being with quite different characteristics from the ocean-racing machines while others, mainly in smaller sizes, still went for a compromise between the types.

Some owners of ocean racers, usually of the larger custom-built variety, still insist that their boats contain the amenities and use them for cruising between races. These are relatively rare, however, and except for a local club race with social overtones, you will seldom find the large true cruising boats trying to mix with the hotshots in competition. It would be like entering the Indianapolis 500 in the family sedan.

The major reason that the split developed was not, from a design standpoint, because of all the provisions of the measurement rule used for handicapping, but because a boat intended for topflight competition should have the greatest possible weight of accommodations and appointments concentrated amidships, keeping the ends of the boat as light as possible. Weight in the ends makes a boat pitch up and down more readily, cutting down on performance—a "hobbyhorsing" boat will not slice through the waves as efficiently. A small difference in hobbyhorsing potential can make all the difference in a race, and designers of ocean-racing boats concentrate their efforts on this characteristic. A cruising boat, however, should use as much available space as possible for accommodations and stowage, including the ends. The fact that top speed will be slowed slightly is not of the same degree of importance as it is in a racing boat, and the intelligent compromise in a cruising boat is to use space first as long as performance isn't ruined.

This one situation alone was enough to prevent the good old-fashioned, husky cruising boat from doing anything in competition against the weight-oriented machines, but there are other factors as well that present an almost irreconcilable problem for someone wanting to have his cake and eat it too in a cruiser-racer.

The pendulum therefore took a strong swing in the early 1970s toward what is known as the full-cruising auxiliary. A distinctive type of boat developed that has become very popular and for pure comfort goes far beyond the "healthy cruising boat" of the 1920s—1960s which could also be used for racing. Much better use than ever before is being made of available space, modern power plants, and rigging techniques to produce boats that are real "cruising machines" as opposed to the "racing machines" they no longer try to compete with.

This category starts at about 30 feet, or perhaps a bit smaller, and goes up close to 60 feet. Most of the boats over 50 feet are custom built. The stock full-cruising boats concentrate in the middle range, with 35–45 being the most popular. More of a compromise is possible under 30 feet. In this range boats are more often used for both cruising (or daysailing) and racing. Many of the small auxiliaries offered by stock builders have a good turn of speed combined with comfort below. In the smaller boats accommodations are not as heavy, and there is no room for such items as showers, deep freezes, and fancy galleys. The cruising accommodations possible in a smaller boat are not so incompatible with speed. There is no space to put a roomy, heavily furnished cabin right across the stern as in the bigger full-cruising boats, and a racing rig isn't too hard to handle for cruising, either. The split isn't so pronounced in this range, but there have been more and more pure racing machines developed in it recently.

A peculiar boat-buying psychology used to puzzle manufacturers of auxiliaries. An owner would not buy a boat unless the model had a good racing record, even though he never intended to race seriously and only wanted the boat for cruising. The chance for name dropping and snob appeal had something to do with it, and manufacturers were often nonplussed by the paradox. Gradually, however, the illogic of this reaction seeped through to the public, and more potential buyers were made aware that they were paying for qualities they would never use.

When we signed up for *Mar Claro* in 1957, it was a reasonable expectation that she would be comfortable for cruising and would also race well, and this turned out to be true. Now a boat bought with this dual role in mind might still do fairly well at both if she were under 30 feet, but it is harder to make the compromise work.

One other point about the dual role is that the gear needed to equip a boat thoroughly for racing adds greatly to her expense. There is no point in trying to race without a full complement of light sails, spinnaker gear, and special winches, along with a great many extra blocks, shackles, and lines. All these cost money and are not needed for cruising. If we had bought now a racing boat for the same base price as our Morgan Out Island 36, the gear to fit her out for topflight campaigning would have increased the base price by 70–80 percent instead of the roughly 15 percent that cruising options added.

For the rest of this chapter, we will assume that the boat is being bought with cruising as the main object, and the analysis of hull forms, rigs, and layouts will be from that point of view, even if she is a type that may also be raced on occasion. We will also assume that there is still the desire for satisfying performance under sail. As long as there has been the expense of spars and sails, they might as well be of good use. There is a type of motor-sailer that is really a slow motorboat with a steadying rig that can only sail if headed downwind in a hurricane, but there is not a large demand for this category.

Hull Forms

A cruising hull should be reasonably roomy for the length—that is, it should have a wide beam carried well aft with good headroom possible, but it should not be a big box. In a given length a box is roomier than something with shape, but in a boat the advantages stop there. Performance that will give pleasure should be a requirement. The first time we took *Tanagra* out, having piously declared our disinterest in racing, we immediately found ourselves checking how she was doing with the other boats around us. We weren't ready to go out and buy extra winches and a spinnaker, but it was still a basic pleasure to see her hold her own in surrounding company. Also, there are many occasions when it's simply a nice feeling to get somewhere under sail and to do it in reasonably good time.

A cruising hull should certainly be seakindly. It should adapt well to waves and chop and should be able to ride out rough weather safely through inherent good design. An easy motion at sea adds greatly to cruising pleasure. Steering should be easy and with positive control. No one wants to fight a wheel or tiller all day, and the location of the rudder well aft, attached to a long keel or with a good skeg in front of it, helps assure this. As for wheel versus tiller, a wheel is more expensive and it seems a luxury in smaller sizes, but it gives more positive control with less effort in larger sizes, and of course allows more room in the cockpit. Some people, including myself, like the feel of a tiller up to about 30–35 feet, and then the easier work of handling a wheel over that range.

This question of seakindliness and control was another factor that led to the distinct cruiser-versus-racer split. In racing boats a designer tries to cut down on wetted surface in the hull to reduce friction and drag, which sometimes leads to very small, short keels and separate rudders, and the result can be a cranky boat that is fast only in the hands of an expert helmsman who concentrates constantly. A cruising man likes to be able to check the chart, light a cigarette, or look at a passing gull without having the boat pirouette out of his hands.

Draft is another consideration. Deep draft can add to seakindliness and general comfort, but it also can limit the areas in which a boat can operate. For this reason, shoal draft is usually considered an asset in a cruising boat. On the Pacific Coast and in Maine, no one worries much about draft, because the coastlines are steep-to, without shoal estuaries and bays. But in southern New England, New Jersey, the Chesapeake, the Carolinas, Florida, the Gulf of Mexico, and in some parts of the Great Lakes, shoal draft is a definite plus. This can mean a shallow hull with a fairly long keel to act as lateral plane. This is not as efficient in keeping a boat from making leeway as is a deeper, shorter keel, and the boat will come about more slowly, but it will do for a cruising boat.

Centerboarders are also popular for cruising in some areas, and that was one reason we chose the Out Island 36. She has a hull form that was originally designed as a racing boat before the IOR changed the emphasis to boats with short, deep keels, and pinched-in ends. The design has a long keel with a centerboard in it. She will sail in shallow water, and when going to windward in deep water will get extra help from the board.

The draft of a boat should be governed by an owner's own requirements, but as a rule, draft of more than 4½ feet is fairly deep for cruising in most areas, and under 3 feet is unusually shallow. The best range is from 3½ to 4½.

Almost all fiberglass cruising hulls are round-bottom, as there is no real advantage to be gained from a V-bottomed hull in a cruising sailboat except for cheaper construction in wood. *Mar Claro*'s strip-planked underbody was round but flared out to a hard chine to join the plywood topsides. This was an economy measure that also provided an unusually good hull form, but this was only so with wooden construction.

Rigs

Leaving out such exotic and rarely found types as a cat ketch or proa (a native South Sea Island type in which the rig is end-for-ended while tacking), the choice in rigs is between single stick and divided. Single stick means catboat, sloop, or cutter, and divided means yawl, ketch, or schooner.

CATBOAT

The single-masted catboat makes a good small cruising boat because of the great beam that goes with the design. (Our Sanderling is 8½ feet wide for 18 feet overall length.) This means a lot of room and good stability, and the mast doesn't interfere with the cabin space. The disadvantage is that the single sail has to be quite big for the size of the boat and is tough to handle in heavy weather. It is difficult to reef while under way, and a cat also tends to have a heavy weather helm on reaches and runs in a breeze, which can make the helmsmanship tiring (although a gaff rig, as previously described, can be "scandalized" quickly). There are bigger cats, but I wouldn't recommend over the midtwenties as a good size for a cruising cat; 22 feet really seems big enough to me.

SLOOP OR CUTTER

As explained in the definitions in Chapter 5, there is no official demarcation between a sloop and a cutter rig, and the argument about just what constitutes one or the other has been a running gag in sailing circles for years. In general, people say a boat is a cutter when her foretriangle is large and the mast is stepped almost in the middle of the boat. This usually means that she carries more than one headsail.

For cruising purposes there isn't much difference between them except that a double headrig gives more flexibility in sail combinations and the mainsail might be a bit smaller on a cutter and therefore a bit easier to handle.

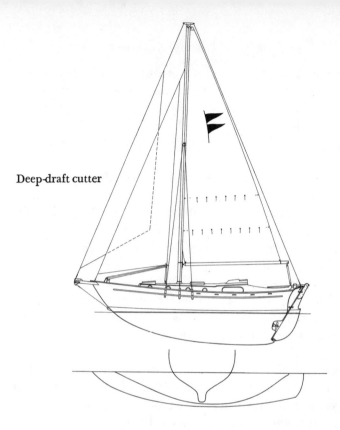

Deep-draft cutter

In the Out Island 36 we had the option of a sloop or ketch, and we took the sloop for several reasons. First of all, we didn't have to pay for all the extra spars, rigging, and sail. Secondly, 36 feet hardly gives you enough length to have all that rig around you, and the mizzen would have to be a rather small, inefficient sail. What used to be the main advantage of the divided rig, the ability to reduce sail gradually and to have some sail up for control of the boat if the main had to be lowered in a blow, has been taken away by the invention of the roller-furling jib. This handy device permits almost instant rolling up of the jib on its own headstay, like a window shade; this provides a quick reduction of sail, and no one has to leave the cockpit. It is even easier than the old expedient of dropping down to jib and jigger (mizzen sail). It does not permit partial reduction of jib area, however. Some manufacturers of roller gear try to sell this feature, but the jib can only have an efficient shape in its full area, and partial rolling is not advisable except in an outright emergency.

Roller-furling mainsails have also been developed. They lack something in aerodynamic efficiency, but they are a great convenience and a safety factor in that the entire rig can be controlled directly from the cockpit—another argument against the added expense, weight, windage, and clutter of a divided rig.

The larger the boat, the more sense it makes to have a divided rig. Over 45–50 feet a single mast has to be pretty tall with a consequently bigger mainsail. For ease of handling, it then might be advisable to split the rig.

YAWL

The modern yawl rig is mainly a racing rig that has varied in popularity depending on how it is treated by the measurement rule in effect. Its main advantage in racing is in the opportunity to add more sail downward via a mizzen staysail or spinnaker. The small jigger on a yawl is not much help either in a jib and jigger "emergency" or in going to windward except as a balancer tending to drive the stern off and, therefore, as a reaction, making the boat point a bit closer; but the yawl rig has no really valid advantages for cruising.

KETCH

The ketch rig, in which the mizzen is forward of the rudderpost and generally larger than a yawl's mizzen, has been popular for cruising for many years, and it does have several advantages. If you do not have a roller-furling jib, or even if you do, the jib and jigger combination can be

very comfortable and easy to handle off the wind in a
blow. With the main down, the boat will be much safer
and easier to control, and should it come to a still heavier
blow, the jigger is relatively easy to take down. Before
the wind in light air, those who like to play with sail combinations can put up mizzen staysails or spinnakers and
increase the boat's sail area.

Several times while cruising in ketches in warm weather
and direct, hot sunlight, we have rigged an awning over
the mizzen boom to shade the cockpit and give us "back-
porch sailing" under main and jib. In the Out Island 36,
though, we have a Bimini top that can be rigged over the
center cockpit while under sail.

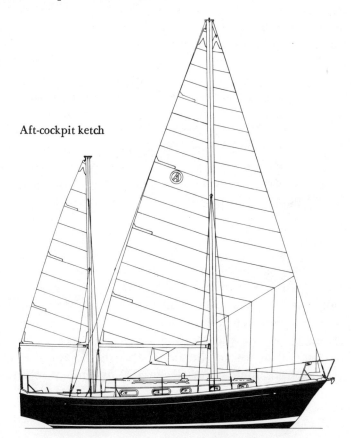

Aft-cockpit ketch

A ketch isn't supposed to be as close-winded as a yawl or sloop for going to weather, but a good ketch rig can provide perfectly good performance and it will no doubt have its devotees for years to come.

SCHOONER

The schooner is the oldest, most traditional rig, very much the dominant one when the cruising boat first gained popularity in the years after World War I, mostly with copies of fishing schooners. Today it is a romantic's rig, and there is little justification for all the extra gear it requires unless you are a traditionalist who likes to have a boat look like a little ship and a reminder of a bygone era. The schooner rig takes more crew to handle than any other and is much more work. It does present the opportunity for a lot of sail combinations and a lot of sail drill if that's what you like, but none of it is very practical anymore.

I will admit, though, that some of the best sails I've ever had have been in schooners on a broad reach in a good breeze. There is a sweep and a swoop to the way a schooner feels under these conditions that other rigs can't quite match, but you pay for the feeling in most other ways. Except for localized, semi-custom builders, you would be hard put to find a new schooner for sale.

Layouts and Accommodations

It is amazing how many variations there can be in getting a few bunks, a head, and some cooking and eating space, along with a place from which to sail the boat, into the relatively few feet of a cruising sailboat. The ways of fitting in bunks, the location of stowage, the galley arrangement, access to the head, and the location of the cockpit have undergone all sorts of ingenious solutions

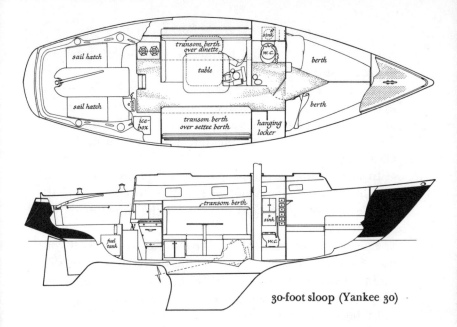

30-foot sloop (Yankee 30)

and, as in almost everything else to do with a boat, some sort of compromise is always involved.

The major sin in the layout department is in trying to put too much in the boat. In an attempt to appeal to the young, growing family on a budget, manufacturers often try to persuade the buyer that they have a "five-sleeper" at 22 feet, or some such, and it is a pathetic claim that will never work. There can always be exceptions, but I would say a general rule of thumb would have it that a boat should only have permanent cabin accommodations for two people up to 22 feet; for four from 22 to 28; for five to 30; and for six from 30 to 40 or larger. These are all maximum limits, and makeshifts can be made for overnight or a weekend that wouldn't work on a longer cruise. Cockpits can be used in good weather or with a tent. Sometimes three children can fill in for two adults. We used to manage *Mar Claro* with five when the children were in their early teens, but only for short jaunts. After a day or two there would be no place in the cabin where it was possible to put a foot down.

When a layout requires double use of space for sleeping and eating, the difficulties are compounded. Everyone is bumping elbows and pushing by each other, and the group must be on tolerant, intimate terms for it all to work.

In small boats for two people, there isn't much variation possible in the basic layout of two V berths fore and aft, a galley on one side, and a head on the other near the hatch to the cockpit.

The first expansion of this layout can come with the use of quarter berths. A quarter berth extends from the cabin aft under the cockpit seats, so that usually only the sleeper's head is out in the cabin. The head and galley must be combined on one side or placed a bit forward to give access to the quarter berths, which naturally cut down on storage space under the cockpit seats. But quarter berths are the most efficient way to add bunk space in a small boat. *Mar Claro* had partial ones that were very comfortable. For about 4 feet, they served as main cabin settees in the daytime, and only the sleeper's feet were poked in under the cockpit. This still left some stowage space there. We also made the compromise of placing the toilet under a removable section of the after end of a big platform double bunk that filled the forepeak. Its extra size made that bunk very comfortable (until someone routed you out in the middle of the night, an emergency that was usually taken care of by a bucket instead) and left space for a good ice chest and hanging locker to starboard, opposite a galley area to port at the forward end of the quarter bunks.

Some people prefer to have the galley right at the cockpit hatch for better communication with the cockpit, but this makes it difficult to fit in quarter berths and also

Facing page: 46-foot tri-cabin sloop or ketch (Cal 2–46)

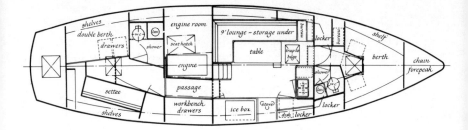

shelves
double berth
drawers
engine room
shower
seat hatch
engine
9' lounge – storage under
table
bureau
locker
bureau
shelf
berth
chain
forepeak
passage
settee
shelves
workbench
drawers
ice box
stove
dish
locker
locker
trap to
bilge
shower
lav.
t.w.c.
lav.

C 2·46

impedes traffic through the hatch. Someone's always putting a foot in the salad just as the cook is adding a sliced egg.

We cruised on a 28-foot sloop once that had the galley counter all the way across the after end of the cabin, with the ladder to the cockpit crossing it. It was such a big expanse of formica that it was impossible to work on it under way. Everything slid merrily back and forth like skaters on a rink.

Headroom is of vital importance on a cruising boat, and it is the subject of some compromise under 28 feet or so. If the cabin is made high enough to provide 6 feet of headroom, the average small boat looks like a dowager in a Queen Mary hat. *Mar Claro* had a convertible hood, which worked very well, except one never lasted more than three seasons. It was not handsome and it would not be a good device for long passages offshore; but it was a very practical solution, and it could be removed or the sides could be rolled up in good weather, doubling the effective cockpit size.

Other providers of small-boat headroom have been the pop-top and the expandable hatch. A pop-top is a permanent, solid cabin top that fastens in place while under way. In port or in calm weather, the fastenings can be unlatched and the top propped up like a bridge table. Side curtains can be added for protection from rain and bugs. The expandable hatch uses the same principle for a large hatch at the after end of the cabin, providing headroom over the galley area.

Headroom is naturally easier to achieve in a deep-hulled boat than in a shoal centerboarder or swing-keel boat, but most smaller cruising boats are of the latter variety and some compromise must be made, unless the crew is content to stoop or sit whenever in the cabin. This is all right for a while but does get tiresome for long cruises.

Center-cockpit tri-cabin sloop or ketch (Columbia 45)

The tri-cabin layout has become extremely popular in the new breed of cruising auxiliary over 35 feet or so, and it makes a great deal of sense. After cruising in four different tri-cabin boats, we decided it was what we wanted when we ordered *Tanagra*. The main advantage is the privacy provided, especially for two couples. With cabins in the bow and stern, each with a head and both used only for sleeping, and the galley-dining area in between as a main cabin, that battle for the multiple use of space is avoided. The dinette can be converted to a double berth when six are aboard, but the setup is really ideal for four. Depending on the size of the boat, this center cabin can be explained into a luxurious lounge or even placed in a raised or semi-raised deckhouse. A popular feature of this type, especially in bad weather, is a passageway under the cockpit from the main cabin to the after stateroom. No need to put foul weather gear on to go about 10 feet.

The tri-cabin layout also means that the cockpit will be under the main boom. Although the term is "center cockpit," it is usually about one-third of the way from the stern. One big advantage is the opportunity to rig a bimini top as mentioned before, and the only drawback is the fact that a bit more spray finds its way in than it would to a cockpit all the way in the stern. This can be overcome with a windshield or dodger.

Until recently, this layout was seen only in real motor-sailers (more motorboat than sailboat), but the full-cruising auxiliary has added a new concept and new dimension to the field.

To recap, general layout considerations include not trying to cram in too much, and making sure that there is plenty of stowage space, that ventilation is good, that the bunks are big enough, and that the galley arrangement is efficient.

Power

In auxiliaries the same choice of gasoline versus diesel applies, and there is also the question in smaller boats of whether to have an outboard motor or an inboard. In smaller sizes, perhaps up to about 26 feet, I think that an outboard motor is the best compromise. There were comments on this in Chapter 7 in relation to daysailers that also apply to small auxiliaries. An outboard is simpler, cheaper, and more reliable as a power plant in smaller sizes. It also leaves much more room in the main living areas of the boat. The only major consideration is whether to have a well or a bracket. If a well is properly designed so that there is enough air for the motor to function, and water does not slosh up and inundate the well, it is a better setup. Different well designs have been developed and several are successful. The major point is to make sure that the motor has enough air to run smoothly. Low horsepower is usually very effective. A sailboat hull is easily driven, and the biggest size that should be used in an auxiliary installation for boats of 24–28 feet is about 9½ horsepower. If you plan extended cruising, take along a couple of extra gas tanks in case you end up in an area where fuel stops are few and far between.

On the question of diesel versus gasoline, there are some excellent gasoline motors in the 25-horsepower range that make fine auxiliary power plants, but I think that diesel is really the answer. Almost all full-cruising auxiliaries are now diesel powered, especially from 30 feet up. Not too long ago, there were no diesels small enough for boats under this range, but there have been recent developments in small diesels that have made them available and practical for much smaller boats.

The two keys to the choice of diesel are safety and reliability. By their nature, diesels fit both of these requirements very well. There is the question of the diesel odor and the initial cost is higher, but the general efficiency of operation, along with the safety factor, are usually the clinchers. The 40-horsepower motor in *Tanagra* uses about three-quarters of a gallon an hour at a cruising speed of about 7 knots. With good tankage, which along with water capacity is important in a well-found cruising boat, she has a range of over 400 miles.

These factors—diesel engine and extra tankage for fuel and water—are added reasons why the split between cruisers and racers has become wider and wider. It is more and more difficult to reconcile the basic needs of the two types. An increasing number of owners wants to go all out in either one direction or the other.

Equipment

Many of the comments that have already been made in the preceding chapter on cabin cruisers apply here. Cruising sailboats almost all come under Classes 1, 2, and 3 in the Coast Guard regulations with the same provisions as powerboats, and they must of course have the proper lights for their type. The main difference is the requirement for a combination bow light under 26 feet and individual red-and-green running lights over 26 feet.

The same recommendations also apply to basic gear such as anchor and line, fenders, mooring lines, first-aid kit, boat hook, and the like. Anchors for cruising auxiliaries deserve a special mention, and again this is one of the main differences between cruisers and ocean racers. One of the joys of cruising is to have an anchor that is easy to handle, which means one that is stowed on the deck forward and easily dropped and weighed. In a racing boat this weight should be kept out of the ends until actual anchoring takes place, but a popular rig on cruising boats from the 30-foot range up is a plow anchor that stows in a special chock forward and need never be wrestled on board. *Tanagra* has one, a 35-pounder, and it works beautifully. There should be a shot of chain about 12–15 feet on the anchor and then a nylon rode. For a spare, the Danforth type is the best answer. It is easily handled and has great holding power once it digs in. Marine chandleries have charts that list the proper weight of anchor and size of anchor line for a given size of boat.

The same basic list that applies to cabin cruisers also can be used for auxiliaries for equipment that is absolutely necessary: radio, flares, flashlights and spotlight, tool kit, engine and rigging spares, binoculars, charts and navigation equipment, swimming ladder, galley gear, ashtrays, foul-weather gear and spare windbreaker, sunglasses, flags and burgees, tide and current tables, dinghy (with an outboard), swabs and sponges, bedding, towels, extra cushions. As an example of just how extensive this list can be, here is the inventory for the charter yachts operated in the Caribbean by the firm of Caribbean Sailing Yachts.

Equipment List

Anchor rodes, 150',
  5/8" Nylon, 2
Anchors
  13-lb. Danforth,
    emergency
  20-lb. plow on
    Capri 30 and 40
  35-lb. plow on
    Carib 41 and 39
  5-lb. plow for
    dinghy
Ammeter
Anemometer, pocket
Ashtrays, beanbag
Awning, Dacron,
  cockpit
Backstay, insulated
  for radio antenna
Baskets, plastic with
  handle, 2
Batteries, 2 sets of 2
  12V
Battery, switch

Bilge, pump, hand
Binoculars, 7 x 50
Blankets, Dacron for
  all bunks
Boat hook
Books
  CSY Manual
  Chapman's
    Guide to Ma-
    rine Life
    Challenge of
    the Sea
Bow chock, mahog-
  any, and roller
  for anchor
Brushes
  Long handled
  Scrub
  Whisk broom
Chafing gear on lines
Charcoal grill
Clothes hangers
Clothespins

Compass
Courtesy flag
Cushions, cockpit
Cushions, life pre-
  server, 4–6
Dishcloths, 2
Dish locker
Dock lines
Dynaplates
Electric bonding
  system
Fenders, set of 3 Par,
  air and line
Fire extinguisher
First-aid kit
Fishing rods, reels,
  and line
Flares, hand, emer-
  gency
Flashlights, 3
Flippers, masks, and
  snorkels
Fly swatter

Fog bell
Fuel filter, extra-large Fram on fuel line
Fuel measuring stick
Funnel, fuel, with strainer
Funnel, water
Galley equipment
  Beer-can opener, stainless steel
  Butter box and cover
  Chore Girls
  Coffeepot
  Corkscrew
  Double boiler and lid
  Frying pan
  Funnel, plastic
  Glasses, red plastic, 6
  Glasses, Tupperware, 6
  Handy Butler
  Ice pick
  Insulated glasses, coffee, 6
  Juice container and top, 36-oz.
  Juice container and top, 50-oz.
  Juice squeezer
  Knife, large
  Knives, paring, 2
  Melmac plates 8″, 6
  Melmac plates 10″, 6
  Melmac soup bowls, 6
  Mixing bowls, large
  Mixing bowls, small
  Peeler
  Pot holders, 2
  Sponges, cellulose, 2; galley, 2
  Sugar bowl
  Tableware, 6 each knives, forks, teaspoons, tablespoons, stainless steel
  Toaster
  Turner
  Utensil box
Genoa sheet gear, including track and fair-lead blocks
Handrails on cabin roof
Ice bag
Insect repellent
International navigation lights
Jerry jugs for extra water
Lead line
Life preservers, horseshoe and bracket by Ulmer
Light bulbs, extra
Lightning grounding system
Mattresses, seat cushions on each bunk
Mirror, head
Mooring cleats
Mop, cellulose
Muffler, stainless steel
Navigation gear
  Necessary charts
  Dividers
  Parallel rulers
  Pencils
Oars and oarlocks for skiff
Oil-pressure gauge
Outboard motor on skiff, new Johnson 4 hp.
Pillowcases
Pillows, foam
Radiotelephone, 65W Bendix
Roller-furling gear for jib
Roller reefing, main boom
Screens
Scuppers (through-deck)
Sheets for berths
Signal horn
Skiff
Speakers, for stereo tape deck, 2
Stereo tape deck and choice of 4-track stereo tapes
Stern pole and ensign
Strainer, fuel
Swimming ladder
Tool kit
  Extra fuses
  Nuts and bolts
  Nylon cord
  Plastic tape
  Tool set
Towels, supply of large and medium
Tow rope, ½″ polypropylene, for skiff
Valves, fuel shut-off
Ventilators, engine-room to meet C.G. requirements
Wall plaques
Washcloths
Wind scoop, Dacron, on forward hatch for hyperventilation

When *Tanagra* was ordered, the options that had to be specified to the builder were hull, deck and bottom colors, centerboard, opening ports in after stateroom, tinted Lucite hatches, pedestal steering and engine controls, extra water tankage, strip teak cabin sole, extra battery, masthead light, spreader lights, electric bilge pump, hot water system, extra shower (in forward head), anchor bow chock, stern pulpit, double lifelines, lifeline gate, quick reef hardware for mainsail, roller-furling hardware for jib, sails and sheets, bimini top, cockpit cushions, windsail ventilator, and genoa winches. And she was then outfitted with most of the equipment that appears on the CSY list above.

As for electronics, sailboats can get away with a weather radio or can go right on up to all the equipment a fancy powerboat would carry, plus some special sailboat goodies like indicators for wind speed and apparent wind, and speedometers. These are not as vital to a cruising boat as to an ocean racer, but they are nice to have if you want the responsibility of keeping them working.

Check the list on electronic equipment available for cabin cruisers at the end of the previous chapter and follow the same bit of advice. Decide what you really need before loading your boat with it. Remember, it all adds to the final cost.

10

Ξ

Racing Sailboats: One Design

The small racing sailboat is the backbone of competitive sailing. Local clubs on both coasts and across the country on lakes, ponds, and rivers sponsor races for a great variety of classes and types, and there is also the "big time" national and international competition right on up to the Olympics. Most of the races are run off on a boat-for-boat basis without handicap for boats with the same dimensions and specifications. These are known as one designs, and most of the familiar classes fall into this category. There are some classes, notably those operating under the international rule that creates the "meter" designation, in which the boats must fit within certain dimensional limits but do not have to have exactly the same hull lines. These are called development classes.

In both cases, no handicaps or time allowances are used—the first boat across the finish line is the winner. Sometimes local clubs will start a mixed bag of different-sized one designs and will use a simplified handicapping system to enable them to race against each other, but the bulk of small-boat racing is boat-for-boat.

The line between "daysailer," as discussed in Chapter

6, and a one-design racing boat is not a distinct one. Many boats that can be used for pleasant, comfortable daysailing can also be raced. The split between nonracing and racing is not as sharply drawn as between cruising boats and ocean racers. As long as boats are of the same design, they can provide enjoyable, close competition. Our catboat, *Polly,* is a good example. She was actually designed as a small cruising boat with two bunks and a head in her cuddy cabin, but we use her only for daysailing and racing. Though she wasn't intended for racing, she sails well enough to furnish good competition. In our club there are a dozen or so of the 22 owners of Sanderlings who want to race, and the competition is as close and intense as if we were in an Olympic class. All the boats are from the same builder, the sails are made by the same firm, and everybody uses the same fittings and equipment. We have all agreed to no "souping up" or altering of the identical boats, and this is true one-design racing. The outcome depends on how the boats are sailed. The closeness of the competition is the key, not the speed of the boats in relation to other classes (which actually isn't bad).

Competition

If you are looking for a boat for one-design racing, you should go about it a bit differently from the search for a daysailer or cruising boat. Your main concern should be to get into good competition, and your choice of boat will probably be governed by the classes that are actually racing in your area. An explanation of how small-boat racing is organized might help explain this point.

It is sponsored in several different ways and by different types of organizations. One chain of command starts with local clubs and proceeds via local yacht-racing associations to regional groupings and from there up to the North

American Yacht Racing Union (NAYRU). NAYRU, which is affiliated with the International Yacht Racing Union (IYRU), a worldwide administrative and rule-making body, sets the rules (in accordance with IYRU rules) by which racing is conducted in North America and sanctions most formal competition. It also conducts individual championships for men, women, juniors, single-handlers, and match racing.

The individual clubs are almost all private membership organizations with the same social structure as a country club, beach club, or any other group with a common purpose. Some are difficult to get into, with waiting lists, high initiation fees, and a complicated sponsorship process, but these are in the minority. If there is an old-line club with all these social entanglements, there is almost bound to be a more informal one nearby with much more flexible entrance requirements. Many sailing clubs are community affairs easily accessible to anyone with an interest in the sport.

Investigate the clubs in your area and find out which one presents the best opportunity for getting the kind of competition that interests you. Once you have this settled, go about choosing the class of boat from those in use there. Pick a boat whose characteristics suit your pocketbook, your skills, and the number of crew available to sail with you. Don't buy a boat first because you like her looks or because you got a good deal. You may end up scouting around in vain for a club to race her.

This leads to the other part of the organization of small-boat racing. Anyone can start a one-design class. There is no sanction needed from NAYRU or any other organization. In our free enterprise system anyone can go into the business of designing, building, and selling a one-design boat. There are those who complain that there are too many classes, leading to confusion, duplication of interest, and a weakening of existing classes, but no one has the right to tell you that you can't do it. Once a class is established in a few fleets, the usual practice is to form a class association. Sometimes this is controlled by the builder, but more often the owners take over and control the plans and specifications, protecting the one-design characteristics of the class so that racing remains even and the boat's resale value is maintained. Our son, Robby, had a Comet, a 16-foot racing sloop, that was 7 years old when he acquired her in 1956, and the same boat is still racing and doing well under her latest owner, competing against boats that are brand new. Some class associations are big enough to have a full-time paid administrator; others are run by volunteers.

Class organizations also conduct their own regional, national, and in some cases international championships for which boats must qualify in local elimination series. In a few cases individual owners who are not members of a local club simply join the class organization and go on the circuit to various class regattas. This is one way of getting started, but a comparatively rare one.

In general, if you want to race, you can certainly find some way of doing it. There are very few areas in North America where sailboat competition is not at hand in some form.

This is the structure of the sport. Now how about the boats? As I said above, there are a great many classes, perhaps too many, and this is a source of some confusion. An advantage, however, is that they cover just about every type of boat imaginable. The classes have names of birds, animals, heavenly bodies, fish, speed synonyms, designers, and sometimes just a number that refers to a dimension, such as sail area, waterline, or overall length.

They are all catboats or sloops and most of them are monohulls, though a few catamaran classes have leaped to wide popularity in recent years.

The Hobie Cat, built in California, hit a mass market at the right time in the late 1960s. It also set a precedent in the sponsorship of competition. The class association, controlled by the builder, bypassed local yacht clubs and set up local, regional, and national competitions for owners.

A catalog of all the one-design classes could get out of hand here, but these are the basic types and some of the better-known examples that are racing. There is a major split between so-called high-performance planing boats and displacement boats that have a lower speed potential.

Types

BOARDBOATS

These simple "sailing surfboards," great for learning and for bathing-suit fun, as pointed out in previous chapters, are also fun for competition. The Sailfish and Sunfish, manufactured by Alcort, were the pioneers of this type and the Sunfish Class remains highly organized, with a host of regattas for owners. Some are club sponsored and others are open to all owners.

Boardboat competition is wet, therefore chilly, except in the best weather, and is usually singlehanded, though "doubles" events are also held. The equipment is simple, performance is good and stimulating, and sailing one of these boats well in a good breeze can be hard work and an athletic challenge. Many junior programs are conducted on boardboats. In some regattas several categories of competition are included, such as men, women, juniors, novices, and doubles, and one boat can provide multiple competitive opportunities, all for a relatively low investment.

Dinghies

Small sailing dinghies, 10 or 11 feet and under, are used for competition at many levels. Junior programs use such dinghies as Sabots, El Toros, and Turnabouts for instruction and racing while some of the top adult skippers, champions with larger boats, dinghy race in the off-season to keep their hand in and polish their skills. Frostbiting (winter dinghy sailing) started on Long Island Sound in 1932 and has spread to many other areas where solid ice is not a problem. (In more northern areas with solid ice, many wet-water sailers take to ice boating in the winter. This is a very special sport that is limited to a few areas by nature.) Short dinghy races provide a concentrated dose of starting and buoy-rounding tactics—and permit the heavily clad sailors to warm up in between. Dinghy equipment is relatively simple and the concentration on tactics is one of the main attractions of this type of sailing.

Singlehanders

A phenomenon of the early 1970s was the advent of a boat called the Laser, sort of a combination of boardboat and dinghy. With more of a boat hull than the surfboard configuration of a boardboat but sportier than a dinghy, this 14-foot, 130-pound cat-rigged racer filled such an obvious need as a second boat for experienced sailors, and as an exciting challenge for juniors and newcomers, that over 6,000 were sold in the first two years.

Singlehanding is a special type of racing that doesn't appeal to everyone, although it does simplify life by doing away with any possible crew problems. Best known in this category is the Finn Olympic dinghy, a brute of a boat to sail and only suitable for strong, athletically inclined experts.

TYPICAL ONE DESIGNS: 16-foot catamaran sloop (Hobie Cat); (*facing page*) 18-foot Sanderling catboat, 28-foot Class E Scow

TYPICAL ONE DESIGNS: *(facing page)* 22-foot Star Class sloop, 17-foot
Thistle and 15-foot Windmill; 15½-foot Snipe, Class C Catamaran

CATAMARANS

The Hobie explosion has been mentioned, and this one builder, with a cat-rigged 14-footer followed by a sloop-rigged 16-footer, did an amazing job of popularizing what had been a very special type of boat. Experimental catamarans have been around for years, adapted from centuries-old South Pacific native craft. The design genius of Bristol, Rhode Island, Nathanael Herreshoff, startled the sailing establishment in the nineteenth century with a radical, two-hulled craft. She was immediately outlawed by officials who feared all other boats would be outmoded. It wasn't until 1959 and *Yachting* Magazine's One-of-a-Kind Regatta in Miami, Florida, that a catamaran, the Tigercat, developed by William S. Cox, was able to prove herself on all points of sailing, and not just off the wind, where cats had long been known as fast boats. With her triumph in this regatta, the catamaran was established as suitable for serious racing, and several one-design classes and development categories gained acceptance. The Aqua-Cat gained wide popular acceptance. California has been particularly strong in sponsoring multihull racing, and the Hobies came along to ice the cake. Acceptance of the Tornado Class for the 1976 Olympics was another big step in catamaran development.

Catamarans are extremely fast on reaches, slow on runs, and moderately capable to windward. They provide exhilarating sailing under some conditions, with more emphasis on boat speed than on tactics, as one good burst of reaching speed can wipe out all the inches and feet gained by tactical moves that mean so much in monohull racing. They range in size from singlehandlers like the small Hobie to mammoth development types like the D-Class catamarans of over 30 feet.

CENTERBOARDERS

Many of the most popular classes are small centerboarders that can operate in shallow water, are easy to beach and haul out, and give performance somewhere in the range from straight displacement to semi-planing. The Snipe, developed during the depression as an inexpensive boat for home building, has been around the longest and grown the biggest of this type in numbers. The home-building aspect was eliminated when wood was replaced by fiberglass, but the hard-chine hull is the same one that was easy for home builders to put together. It is a boat that a husband and wife, parent and child, or juniors can sail together, which has accounted for much of its popularity, and it is backed by a strong international organization.

Most two-man centerboarders do not have a spinnaker, since that adds greatly to the need for an experienced crew, and most of them can get up on a plane, or near to it, on a reach in a good breeze.

If a centerboarder is big enough to carry a crew of two in addition to the skipper, it is usually equipped with a spinnaker and is therefore more of a challenge. Introduced in 1939, the 19-foot Lightning is an example of a popular three-man centerboarder that has also spread worldwide under a well-organized class association. It is surprising how much the extra crew member adds to a skipper's difficulties in organizing his racing. Unless one's family provides a ready-made and willing supply of crew members (and if they're not willing, don't force it) this can be a problem and a factor in choosing a class.

Most centerboarders are dry-sailed—stored on land between races—and this is a great advantage in maintenance and convenience. Clubs usually have a power hoist that can pull small boats out quickly for stowage on trailers in a parking yard. A word of warning: be very careful about overhead wires when moving a boat on a trailer. Sailors have been electrocuted when masts or rigging have made contact. A sailboat parking lot should be free of any such dangers.

HIGH-PERFORMANCE BOATS

A step up from the semi-planing or displacement center-boarder is the full-planing boat, one with a light, shallow hull that easily rises to the surface and planes like a fast motorboat in winds of any decent strength. Most of these are centerboarders, though there are a few planing keel-boats, notably the Olympic-class Tempest. The earliest example of the planing hull to come into general use in racing was the scow type, a slipper-shaped hull with rounded or scow bow. Several sizes of scow have been popular on Midwestern lakes since early in the twentieth century and they are still going strong. They have also spread east to shoal water spots like New Jersey's Barnegat Bay, where they revel in the fresh sea breezes.

Scows are sporty and fast for protected-water sailing, with great demands on a crew's quickness and agility. Some of the best sailors in the world have been developed in scow racing. The M-16 is a popular small-sized scow, and the 28-foot Class E scow has been a highly competitive class for over 50 years.

The 19-foot Flying Dutchman, an Olympic class, is an example of a planing boat with a conventional pointed bow with a performance potential similar to the scow's. This class has a trapeze for the crew to increase sail-carrying ability by getting the crew's weight farther out over the side than unassisted hiking could accomplish. It also has a spinnaker, and this means a very active and demanding role for the crew as well as the skipper. The 17-foot Thistle, introduced in the 1940s, did a great deal to popularize light planing boats for club and family racing. Experts can enjoy the challenge of a Thistle but average club sailors can handle them well, too.

KEELBOATS

These are in the minority for small-boat racing because they limit the choice of courses in many shallow-water areas. They are also more difficult to trail and to handle around a launching area. The first one-design class, the Star, introduced on Long Island Sound in 1911, was and still is a keelboat. It has gone through many changes in rig and construction methods and has survived as a very competitive boat, used in the Olympics through 1970, the longest tenure any class has had in the Games. The new Olympic keel class, the Soling, has spread rapidly in recent years. The Star has a crew of two and no spinnaker, while the Soling has three and does use a spinnaker.

Keelboats are usually in the higher cost range for one-design racing, but they have their devotees among those who like to feel "a real boat" under them. Also, of course, they do not capsize as their keels give them stability but, should they knock down far enough to swamp, they will sink since their keels are heavier than any possible flotation.

Equipment

One designs are subject to Coast Guard regulations on life jackets, according to the boat's length. They are not equipped with running lights as a general rule but must have them if they are to be sailed at night.

Equipment for one-design racing is kept to class safety requirements, which usually call for life jackets, anchor and line, bucket, bailer or pump, and a paddle. All these should be selected for lightest possible weight. Coast Guard regulations now permit sensible life vests that can be worn comfortably while racing a small boat, and these should be selected carefully.

The question of equipment in one designs boils down to fittings and "go-fasts," and these vary according to class rules. As I've pointed out, the Sanderling Class in which we race at our club prohibits, by local fleet agreement, anything but standard fittings and hardware, but this is not the case in most other classes.

The dedicated one-design campaigner can become wrapped up in Barber hauls (for adjusting the angle of jib leads), Cunningham holes (for adjusting luff tension on the mainsail), jam cleats, snubbing winches, Hifield levers, traveler assemblies, various types of blocks, halyard locks, turnbuckles, hiking sticks, and all sorts of special items. If you want to keep it simple, stick to a class with rigid one-design rules on gear and equipment. If you are a gadgeteer and like to fuss with new things and improve the efficiency of your rig, one of the gadget-loaded classes like the Flying Dutchman, Star, or Soling might interest you more.

You can make almost anything you want out of one-design racing from dinghy sailing at the local club to fighting for an Olympic berth. And the fascination of it is that you never stop learning. It is a sport of endless challenge.

Racing Sailboats: Offshore

Deep-water sailboat racing is the world's most complicated, sophisticated—and expensive—sport. The complexity of the equipment is unmatched anywhere else, and the organization of a good crew that will get the most out of the equipment is a full exercise in logistics, personnel management, and the psychology of teamwork. An ocean racer is about as expensive per foot as any kind of pleasure craft, perhaps matched only by a luxury sport fisherman, and on no other boat is every inch so carefully planned for one function. The cliché that owners have used to describe what their feelings are in operating an ocean racer is that it is like sitting in a cold shower tearing up $100 bills and shoving them down the drain while feeling nauseated and being pummeled with a club.

The admitted expense and discomfort of the sport would seem to make it a candidate for oblivion but, against all logic, it continues to grow in scope and complexity. New entry records are set almost every time a major offshore event is held, and fancier, glossier, more sophisticated boats are forever joining the lists. The tangible rewards are minor. Fame isn't one of them, as the general public pays very little attention, and the trophies have no monetary value.

The elemental satisfaction of looking back and seeing your competitors behind you is also lacking as often as not. Since most races are sailed as handicap events, you're never sure you have won until the committee has worked out the time-allowance corrections after every boat has finished. In *Mar Claro* we were often the smallest boat in the race, with a good time-allowance handicap, and we would sometimes win a race on handicap when all the other crews were already ashore relaxing in the bar (cutting down somewhat on the dramatic impact of the victory). It is nice to win, but the immediate satisfaction of putting it to the other guy, as in one-design racing, is definitely lacking.

There is also a large element of luck. The best boat with the best crew and the best equipment, well sailed at all times, can be crossed up by the vagaries of the wind or current.

All this negative sales talk is included as a realistic appraisal, yet these factors do not seem to act as a deterrent. The sport continues to grow and flourish. It has existed since 1866, but it was a pastime for millionaire owners, with professional crews doing the sailing until the 1920s. Then in the surge of interest in yachting after World War I, it began to develop on an amateur basis. The revival of the Bermuda Race in 1923 (it had been held before the war for very small fleets on a hit-and-miss basis) was a major impetus. The crews were amateur and the boats were heavy cruising boats out to prove their offshore ability.

Organization and Measurement Rules

The organization of offshore racing is not as well structured as that of one-design racing, although the North

American Yacht Racing Union is becoming increasingly involved. Sponsorship is still mainly by individual clubs. Some races are by invitation but most are open to anyone with the money and inclination.

As explained in Chapter 9, the old role of a combined cruiser-racer has been lost in the intensification of competition in recent years all because of the increased importance of building to measurement rules. To enable boats of different sizes and characteristics to race on a theoretically equal basis, some form of handicapping is naturally necessary, and this has always been done in offshore racing by developing a rating for each boat that is then used in conjunction with a table of time allowances. This table was figured out, basically, over 100 years ago by Nathanael Herreshoff, working in data for the various points of sailing such as beating, reaching, and running, so that a boat rating 30 would give a boat rating 25 so many seconds per mile.

Waterline length is the major element in determining a boat's speed potential, and a simple rating rule taking it and sail area into account would seem to cover the situation. So many variables and subtle elements affect these basic factors, however, that measurement rules over the years have become more and more complicated. For example, the actual effective waterline length can be made very different from the waterline length of a boat at rest by the amount of hull that gets into the water when the boat heels.

A modern measurement rule fills a pamphlet of 25 or 30 pages with formulas, equations, square roots, cosines, and all sorts of higher mathematics, and only a naval architect can fully understand one. As the rules have become refined, building to them has required ever more exacting specifications, gradually doing away with the old cruiser-racer compromise.

Since the adoption of the International Offshore Rule

(IOR) in 1970, the split which had been growing under former handicap systems became virtually complete. Almost all the major events, such as the Bermuda Race, Transpac to Honolulu, the Mackinacs, Southern Ocean Racing Conference, and occasional transatlantic races are conducted under IOR, as are other major events around the world, fostering one type of boat for international competition in all areas. These top events have been organized into a World Ocean Racing Championship sponsored by *Yachting* Magazine.

There are also hundreds of shorter localized events wherever there is enough water to support the boats—even little Eagle Mountain Lake in Texas, as described in Chapter 1. Some are afternoon affairs while others take overnight, a weekend, or several days. Southern California has year-round ocean racing, as does Florida and the Gulf of Mexico, and the really eager competitors move around from area to area by the season.

Boat Types

With this background it is obvious that advice to a newcomer interested in getting into this phase of the sport is a bit different from the advice you would give someone buying an outboard motorboat. The choice of boat is dictated much more by the demands of the measurement rule than the individual wishes of the owner. You may want a yawl rig or a centerboard hull, but the rule might make these choices unwise; and you had better get a deep-hulled sloop if you want to win. This is because the rules never remain static for long. If one type of boat seems to be doing well in comparison to others, the rule may be changed (by a committee of the International Yacht Racing Union) to emphasize different features and supposedly equalize performance of the boats that have been hot.

Through the history of the sport, what was a top-notch type in any one year would soon be "equalized" by the rule, and this practice has continued and will continue.

There are different categories of offshore racing, however, and a rundown of these might be helpful, along with another reminder on expense. There is no way to stint and win in offshore racing. You have to have the equipment. As I've mentioned before, had we decided on a 36-foot ocean racer instead of a cruising boat when we ordered *Tanagra,* our Out Island 36 cruising sloop, the bill for the same size boat equipped for offshore campaigning would have been well over $50,000, instead of $35,000.

Although handicapping ocean racers is set up so that a 3o-footer can in theory compete in the same race with a 70-footer (we were 15th in the Miami-Nassau Race in a 31-footer at the very bottom of the handicap list of 105 boats the year that the 73-foot *Windward Passage* set the course record but ended up 55th on corrected time), there has been a growing tendency recently to compartmentalize offshore racing into groups of roughly similar size boats. Of these, the one for the smallest size boats is the Midget Ocean Racing Club (MORC) category. MORC is a national organization that has its own measurement rule and sanctions local fleets to hold races for boats less than 30 feet overall.

This is one way to beat the high cost of racing. An MORC boat is more expensive than a daysailer or small cruiser of the same size, but far cheaper than the big ocean racers, and, since cruising accommodations are naturally lighter and simpler, an MORC boat can be used for some cruising as well.

Another development that has gained strength recently is called "level racing." This means racing boats of the same rating on a boat-for-boat basis with no time allow-

TYPICAL OFFSHORE RACERS: Morgan 36 One Tonner, Cal 48; (*facing page*) Columbia 57, C&C 61

ance. The boats do not have to be alike, as in one-design racing, just as long as they measure out to the same rating under the IOR or whatever rule might be used. This type of racing was given a boost by international competition for an old trophy that was originally called the One Ton Cup when it was a small-boat trophy early in the century.

It retained its name when reinstated, but the boats used for the competition have no connection with one ton or any other weight as a definitive measurement. Actually they are from about 35 to 40 feet and rate at 27.5 under IOR. The success of One Ton Cup racing has fostered other similar competitions for Quarter, Half, Three-Quarter, and Two Ton designations, again having no relationship to the weight implied by the name other than as a convenient reference. The various Ton boats are now organized into class associations, and categories for them are included in some events in addition to the regattas staged especially for them. Some are from stock builders and others are "one-off" custom jobs.

Stock boats from a single manufacturer also engage in one-design, or level, racing in some areas. This has been particularly true of California where many of the builders of stock ocean racers are located. These boats may race against each other with no handicap in special class events, but they might rate differently when measured for a handicap race. Changes in rig, ballast, type of propeller, and sail area all can alter a stock boat's rating.

The queens of the ocean-racing field are the specially designed custom-built boats by top naval architects such as Olin Stephens, Phil Rhodes, Cuthbertson and Cassian, Bill Lapworth, Gary Mull, Bruce King, Bill Tripp, Alan Gurney, and Britton Chance. Since the days when ocean racers were mainly replicas of fishing schooners, these men have been working to develop faster and faster offshore boats, always under the influence of whatever rule might be in effect. Although custom boats for the smaller Ton classes and MORC competition have been and are being designed, most designer products are in the size range over 40 feet. Years ago, an arbitrary limit of 73 feet was placed on ocean racers when the Cruising Club of America Rule was in effect. This was done to halt a burgeoning building race, since the CCA, which sponsors the Bermuda Race and developed the rule to administer that event, felt that it would change the character of racing to have boats that were too big and too hard to handle in the competition. Since there were some 72-footers then racing, the limit was set one foot bigger and remained there for years. When the IOR came in, a top rating of 70 was chosen to fit the old CCA requirement as closely as possible, and the largest boats are still in the just-over-70-foot range.

Costs

Fiberglass, aluminum, and still occasionally wood are the materials specified, and everything from bunk locations to type of propeller is calculated for its effect on the boat's rating. Weight in the way of bulkheads and interior fittings is usually reduced to the barest minimum, and cruising on even the largest and lushest modern ocean racers can be a Spartan experience.

The price tag? Figure $1,500–$2,000 a foot for the less elaborate boats and something around $500,000 or much more for the big 70-footers.

Aside from architects' fees and premium building costs, these costs run so high because of the special equipment required.

Equipment

Rather than listing equipment as in previous chapters, an overall description may give enough of an idea. First, the boats have to have the legal equipment for their size in the way of lights, fire extinguishers, anchors, etc. Then most of them would have the bulk of the "housekeeping" items listed in Chapter 9, leaving out only such cruising amenities as hibachis and elaborate galley gear.

Beyond these necessities the NAYRU has compiled equipment lists that are required for different categories of offshore events (see Appendix B). For major distance races such as the Bermuda Race, the list covers several pages and is a very thorough catalog of items needed for safety at sea, both for operations and for emergency situations such as man overboard, dismasting, or hull damage.

Finally, the sail inventory of an ocean racer is something like the wardrobe of a movie star—something for every conceivable occasion or maybe several choices for each eventuality. Most of the top competitive boats in an event like the SORC will carry a complement of about 30 extra sails. The mainsail is usually adjustable for different conditions, but the array of genoa jibs for degrees of wind strength, drifters, cheaters, tallboys, and staysails, plus several weights and cuts of spinnakers, adds up to quite an inventory. And this would be on a sloop. Add about 5 or 6 more staysails and a mizzen on the two-stickers.

These are the facts. Do you still want to get into offshore racing? If you do, you are one of a growing number of fanatics who have caught the bug badly despite the harsh realities.

12

Character Boats

Along with the nostalgia craze for old musical shows, old cars, and old radio programs, there has been a turning backward in boating, too. For a combination of sentimental and practical reasons, there is a considerable vogue in what are usually called "character boats" in both sail and power.

Originally, most yachts were adaptations of commercial types. The nineteenth-century ocean-racing boats like the schooner *America* were copied from the swift pilot schooners that were the fastest thing under sail at that time. Later on, fishing schooners were used as models for cruising auxiliaries, and pleasure versions of such workboats as Cape Cod catboats were turned out for yachtsmen.

Gradually, as the demand for yachts grew in the late nineteenth and early twentieth centuries, a few naval architects began to specialize as yacht designers, and the practice of adapting workboats was no longer so prevalent. It has never died out completely, however, and today's boat buyer still has the chance to get into the field.

Very often this is a regional business, fairly well localized, but some workboat types have become generally known and might be encountered almost anywhere, either as genuine antiques or as modern replicas. Here are a few of the better-known ones.

Sail

CATBOAT

We have already talked about the catboat as a pleasure boat, particularly our own 18-foot Sanderling Class *Polly*. She is a modern replica and illustrates how modern materials can be used to improve on the characteristics of an older type. The original catboats were intended for one man to work as a fishing boat with a simply handled rig, shallow draft for operating out of small bays and harbors, offshore ability, and the carrying capacity to handle a good catch of fish. With the mast stepped all the way forward, there was no way that stays could be rigged, so it had to be a big, strong, solid hunk of wood. To support this weight, the bow section had to be broad and flat, and the old catboats weren't too good to windward. In replica boats, the reduction in weight by using hollow aluminum sections for the mast allows a finer bow, and this modern cat goes to windward very well and is drier in the process. She also steers better off the wind without the weight of the old, heavy mast putting torque on the bow.

There has been a real vogue in replica catboats in recent years with several stock builders doing well, and there are also a few genuine antiques lovingly preserved. There is a Catboat Association comprised of owners of both originals and replicas. The type makes great sense as a pleasure boat under modern conditions—owning one is more than just a stunt. The cubic space in their beamy hulls makes them about as much boat as you can get in a given overall length, and the simplicity of rig is a plus.

FRIENDSHIP SLOOP

These boats get their name from the Maine coastal town of Friendship where they were originally built for the type of work the catboat did farther south. They didn't have to be shallow draft to operate out of Maine's deep harbors,

Facing page: a Friendship sloop in Friendship, Maine

but they had to have sailing ability and fish-carrying capacity. Friendships varied in size from around 20 to over 40 feet, and they first came into vogue as yachts during the depression, when the fishermen, switching to powerboats, were sometimes forced to let them go for just a few hundred dollars (they hadn't cost much more than that to build) and smart yachtsmen were looking for bargains. Their distinctive high clipper bows, graceful sheer, and gaff-sloop rig gave them a salty look that was appealing to traditionalists, and they sailed quite well.

Over the years they of course acquired more "character" as conventional yachts went to Marconi rigs and the sleek hulls of ocean racers, and now the originals are highly prized antiques. A few replicas have been built in both wood and fiberglass. As a modern cruising boat, the Friendship leaves something to be desired in cabin accommodations, and the rig has a lot more "strings" than a modern boat; but the sailing ability is still there, and the look is more distinctive than ever against boats of modern design.

Friendship lovers are fanatics and there is no longer a bargain to be found in buying one. The replicas have been expensive to build, and the old ones now have a pretty high price tag, which will go higher as they gradually go out of existence.

BUGEYE
The Chesapeake has fostered several local types that have become popular as yacht conversions and the bugeye is the best known in other areas. These boats, with sharply raked masts either in a ketch rig or of exactly equal height, were developed for the Chesapeake's shallow waters as fishing, oystering, and freight boats with broad shallow hulls, simply built and rigged. These, too, were first picked up by yachtsmen as bargains when commercial owners were forced to sell them and then were copied by yacht

builders, and in some cases, drastically modernized. Not too many of them are left and their chief value now is purely for those who enjoy owning a traditional type. They were an outgrowth of the slender log canoes that were made from one big log. A few canoes still exist on the eastern shore of the Chesapeake as museum pieces.

Single-masted boats of V-bottomed hull form known as skipjacks were also used as Chesapeake workboats and have occasionally been adapted to yacht use. Some of them are still oystering under sail.

SHARPIE

Popular on the Chesapeake but also used in Long Island, Connecticut, New Jersey, and other areas with shallow water, the sharpie is still in existence today, turned out by home builders and regional boatyards because the simple hull provides the longest boat for the least money, along with real shallow-water adaptability. The sharpie hull, which can be almost any size up to 40 feet or more, is really just a big flat-bottomed rowboat, perhaps with a slight dead rise or camber to give the bottom a bit of shape. In larger versions it is rigged as a Marconi ketch, sometimes with leeboards instead of a centerboard to keep the hull construction as simple as possible. Unless a cabin is added, which usually proves ungainly, it can only provide sitting headroom in even the largest sizes. It is not good for offshore work, or even in choppy coastal waters, but the hull is easily driven under sail and by a low-powered outboard for auxiliary. In some areas where a simple, easily driven open boat will fill the bill, sharpie hulls are used as powerboats.

FISHERMAN SCHOONER

As has been pointed out, most early cruising auxiliaries were based on the New England fishing schooners, often

EXAMPLES OF
CHARACTER BOATS:
a fisherman-type
schooner, a trawler-
type powerboat;
(*facing page*) a Jersey
sea skiff, a sharpie
hull used as a
working powerboat,
a rowing dory, a
steam launch version
of a lifeboat

coming from the same yards. The Boston designer John Alden made them particularly famous by winning the Bermuda Race with three of them. He had hundreds built as yachts in Maine yards that had been turning out commercial craft. Gradually, the schooner fell out of favor for ocean racing because the rig is not as close-winded as a sloop or yawl and takes too much work for easy handling while cruising. Very few schooners are being built today, but many of the older ones that have had good care are still around and are eagerly sought by traditionalists. Most of them were built in Maine or Nova Scotia, and one of their problems is that bargain hunters often buy them for cruising to the Caribbean or other southern areas. Unfortunately, the northern woods they were built from frequently do not stand up well in the tropics.

Replicas of the fisherman type or of the smaller coasting schooners that were similar but often had clipper bows instead of spoon bows are still being built, and the old schooners have achieved the status of "classic," especially with the fanatics who love schooners above all. A few romantics have imported Chinese junks but they are more colorful than practical. .

There are, as mentioned above, many localized sailboat types that are preserved as yachts in isolated cases, and it is generally wise to keep them in the waters they were intended for.

Power

TRAWLER

We have already discussed the trawler type that has become extremely popular as an offshore cruiser. The term is not an exact one and has come to mean almost any displacement hull of rugged construction and high freeboard intended for long-range cruising in deep water. The type has been adapted to modern stock-boat production, and these boats can hardly be called classics or even character boats. Many owners have, however, actually bought commercial hulls and made them into yachts, buying old boats and cleaning them up or acquiring a bare hull straight from the commercial builder. The shrimp-boat type popular as a workboat in Southern states has made a good conversion in frequent cases. If you want space, seakeeping ability, a salty, shippy look, and don't care about speed, this is the type for you.

MONTEREY

A true workboat type that has many of the characteristics of the trawler boats, this distinctive California fishing boat shows a strong old world influence. Fishermen whose ancestry went back to the Mediterranean developed the boat for working out of Monterey, San Francisco, and other California ports, not as a copy of any particular boats from the old country, but still showing strong influences such as a clipper bow and marked sheer. Some are double-ended and others have rounded sterns, and they range up to about 40–45 feet. They are heavily built and give good performance in rough water, and knowledgeable yachtsmen have acquired them for conversion when possible, although they are not easy to come by.

JERSEY SKIFF

Until the fiberglass era, this was one of the most popular boats for sport fishing. The breed started on the Jersey Coast, introduced by Scandinavian fishermen whose ancestry went back to the Vikings. The hulls were originally intended for launching through the surf from the beach to tend offshore nets, and were rowed. They had very pronounced sheer, with high bow and stern for the two-way trip in the surf, and were of lapstrake construction, handed down directly from the Vikings. When power came in, the graceful high sterns, great for rowing and for landing through surf, squatted badly under any load of power, and gradually a powerboat hull was developed using the lapstrake construction, high bow and good sheer, and a shallow, hard-bilged, round-bottomed hull form flattened out in the stern. Use of the boats as rum runners taught their operators a lot about speed and about rough-water performance.

There are local builders turning out wooden skiffs still, and there have been fiberglass versions, though it doesn't make much sense to duplicate lapstrake in fiberglass. However, the type will be growing progressively scarcer and a well-preserved Jersey sea skiff could almost rank as a classic by now.

GARVEY

Another localized New Jersey type that has moved out into other areas is the garvey, a flat-bottomed open boat with a turned-up scow bow. It started as a workboat on lower Barnegat Bay, which is extremely shallow, and has been adapted for pleasure use by fishermen and duck hunters. The type has a good turn of speed in smooth water, but is wet and bouncy in a chop. Some models have had a slight amount of dead rise added to the bow section to cut down on the wetness and pounding. The sneak-box, another duck-hunting boat from this area, is a shallow, slipper-shaped boat with pointed bow and is used for moving around the marshes. It was also adapted as a racing sailboat and has been used as a junior trainer in the area for about 75 years.

DORY

The distinctive Grand Banks fishing dory, with a narrow, flat bottom, flared sides, and sweeping sheer, a form functional for nesting several on a schooner's deck, and also for rowing and for carrying a load of fish, has been adapted by some yachtsmen as a utility launch. She makes an easily driven hull—initial stability is poor, but ultimate stability is excellent, making her a good rough-water hull.

These are just a few examples of the character boats in sail and power that make sense as pleasure boats either because their function is still pertinent or because they please a traditionalist's bent for nostalgia, or both. And today's stock boat might just become tomorrow's classic if you treat her with enough tender loving care to last that long.

13

Practical Matters

We have been through the boat types now, and perhaps you have been able to end up with the right boat for you. What next? What else should you be thinking about? You have the recommended equipment, and the boat is ready to go. You still have to make her legal by registering or documenting her, and you need a place to keep her. You should also know how to operate her safely, and she should be insured.

Registration

Most states have their own boat-registration laws, different in each state. In some areas the Coast Guard is still charged with numbering boats when there is no state law, but there are very few of those left. If you buy through a yard or dealer, he will have the information on how to go about registration. If you have bought a boat in another area or from an individual, inquire at any boat dealership about regulations in your state. Some states have operator's licensing requirements for intrastate waters, but there is no license required on interstate waters that are federally controlled, at least as this is being written. There has been agitation for operator licensing, so it may come, but as of now the only license needed is by those operating boats for hire, carrying passengers.

State laws on boat operation vary widely, and you should be familiar with the special laws of any state you intend to operate in. This is especially true in regard to control of overboard discharge of sewage. Federal laws are being promulgated, but the process is a slow one.

Documentation

You might want to investigate documentation of a cabin cruiser or auxiliary sailboat with the Coast Guard as an alternative to registration with a state. States charge annual fees, but there is no charge for documentation. Contact the Coast Guard for information on whether your boat is eligible for documentation. Coast Guard headquarters in Washington, D.C. (400 7th St. N.W., Washington, D.C. 20591) can provide the information if you do not have a Coast Guard installation near you.

Insurance

The right insurance for your boat is very important. Most homeowner policies include liability provisions for boats under 26 feet, and larger boats can be included by paying a small extra premium. The boat itself should be insured against damage and loss by a company that specializes in marine insurance. Many of them advertise in the boating magazines. Small boats and outboard motors may be insured by industry association programs. Information on these is usually included with a new boat or motor and should be investigated. Be sure your policy is worded to give you coverage in the physical areas and in the time period you intend to use the boat. If you go out of an area of coverage or operate out of season, you could unwittingly be uninsured.

Education

Experience is the best teacher, and to gain knowledge and confidence there is no substitute for time on the water but you can prepare yourself ahead of time. The Coast Guard and many states put out safe-boating instructions in simplified form, and every bookstore that carries nautical books has many how-to-do-it titles on boating. And the boating magazines are a continuing source of background information.

Excellent courses in safe boating and boat operation and handling are conducted by two nationwide organizations, the U.S. Power Squadrons (USPS) and the U.S. Coast Guard Auxiliary (USCGA). The USPS is a private organization of yachtsmen dedicated to boating education, and its courses are highly recommended as a starter. They are conducted in local areas, usually in the fall, and cover piloting and seamanship; there is also a sailing course. You should be able to locate your local USPS through boat dealers or yards.

The USCGA is a civilian arm of the Coast Guard, also charged with education and with promoting boating safety as an assist to the regular Coast Guard. The local police station can put you in touch with a Coast Guard Auxiliary flotilla if you have no other way of locating one.

Many adult education programs include boating courses that can be quite helpful, and there are commercial sailing and navigation schools in many areas. Again, most of these advertise in the boating magazines.

The final chapter of this book is a short rundown of basic boating safety—but don't stop there. Take one of the courses mentioned above and do all the reading you can as preparation for getting afloat.

Berthing or Mooring

As the boating population increases, the question of where to keep a boat becomes ever more important. In some areas, particularly Southern California, virtual saturation of waterfront facilities has been reached. The pressures are not quite so great in regions with a greater number of natural harbors and bays.

DRY-LAND STORAGE

Depending on the size of boat, you have quite a few choices. First, of course, is storage at home. This is the cheapest and best solution if the boat can be trailed and if it fits into your type of operation. It limits you in the size of boat and it is only possible if you have space enough where you live. And theft of boats from home storage is quite common. If the boat is on the trailer ready to go, an enterprising pirate can simply hitch her up and drive off, so provide some sort of security if there is any likelihood of this.

Keeping a boat at home makes maintenance easy, and stocking her for a trip is also quite simple. All these advantages should be considered if you happen to be choosing between a trailable and nontrailable boat. Then, too, your choice of horizons is limited only by the distances you want to drive. You can vary your operations between lakes and seashore, experience different kinds of fishing, swimming, and sightseeing, and use the boat as a camper for vacation trips.

If you are a city dweller with no parking space for the boat, a trailed boat can still be kept in storage on land at a yard or marina. Dry storage on or off trailers is increasingly popular with even the largest boats in areas where afloat berthing is scarce. Mobile lifts and cranes make easy launching in a matter of minutes. Small boats are often stored on racks in big sheds, tier upon tier, like loaves of bread on a supermarket shelf, and are moved quickly in and out by forklift tractors. Wooden boats didn't take kindly to this sort of treatment because they dry out, but there is no need for fiberglass or aluminum boats to be in the water when not in use. In fact, they are usually more secure and better protected from storms and high water when they are on land. Bottoms stay clean longer, paint is better protected, and the boat probably won't be as damp as if she were afloat at all times. This all works better with powerboats than with masted vessels, but they too can be handled on land with the proper setup.

At home on the water

Of course a pleasant solution to where to keep a boat is to own a waterfront house. It is really great to have the boat at your doorstep ready to go whenever you are, and there are the obvious advantages of accessibility for maintenance and stocking. A disadvantage is that the boat is entirely your responsibility. In a blow there is no yard crew to help you secure her or move her to a safer spot, and security against theft and vandalism can sometimes be a problem. If you can afford waterfront, though, it is a great feeling to have the boat right there. Just the joy of looking at her is part of the fun of ownership.

Clubs

Membership in a club with its own marina, mooring area, or parking yard can be another answer. It can be an expensive answer at times, but a club has many advantages in addition to providing a place to keep your boat. Competition and organized activities, in addition to the social pleasures of belonging to a group of people with similar interests, are all pluses. There is usually some form of security against theft and bad weather, plus launch service, and, in some cases, other service facilities. Most clubs have fine locations on a good body of water, putting you in the heart of the action right from the start.

MARINAS

Marina living has become an established facet of the boating world, and a major part of the boating population now operates out of marinas. There are marinas—and marinas. Some are just a small collection of slips that could hardly be dignified by the term, in contrast to the vast spreads in such places as Shilshole Bay near Seattle; Long Beach, California; and Fort Lauderdale. Marinas are operated by clubs, municipalities, states, and commercial interests, and getting a slip in one can be a matter of simply walking in and signing up, or of putting your name at the end of a two-year waiting list. This is actually the case in some Southern California harbors.

As noted in Chapter 3, availability of a slip might end up as the deciding factor in your choice of boat. Dealers with marinas attached to their showrooms can use them as a not-so-gentle persuader in congested areas. Whenever a slip becomes available, he will keep it for his own customers instead of letting a stranger move in.

In choosing a marina, if you are able to make a choice, check out some of its features before signing up. In our area of New Jersey, several big new marinas were built in a period in which there were no hurricanes or bad storms for several years. When the first hurricane hit, they proved to be in very exposed spots and badly planned, and many of the boats in them were reduced to matchwood. Look for slips too small for the boats in them, pilings too low so that the boats might ride over them in hurricane tides and then be impaled when the waters recede; look also for improper bulkheading which would allow a heavy surge to develop in rough weather.

Marinas offer many conveniences and amenities. It is nice to have electricity and water connections, shower rooms, laundromats, restaurants, gift shops, and marine services right at hand, and some people enjoy the community feeling of being in a marina. Life can be sociable with much visiting back and forth, and there is always something to look at—a new boat arriving, someone having trouble making a landing, a husband-and-wife fight on the next boat.

Which leads to the disadvantage of marina life. It is like being in a goldfish bowl. Privacy is at a minimum and noise can be a problem, especially on weekend nights when the parties get going. Some marinas have rather strict regulations on conduct while others are wide open. Most of them have security guards. However, the sheer size of the really big ones where it is impossible to check on all strangers, makes such measures ineffective.

Marinas are not cheap either. Rates vary by the area and by the season, with season rentals considerably cheaper than transient rates.

MOORING OUT

In some areas with limited shoreline available for marina installations but plenty of anchorage space, most of the boats ride at mooring. Sometimes these are provided by a club, boatyard, or municipality. Sometimes the owner is responsible for his own equipment. *Mar Claro* sat at a mooring in front of our house for 9 years, tied up at a 150-pound mushroom with a chain and plastic pickup buoy. She broke loose only once, fortunately with wind and tide in a direction to send her harmlessly against a sedge bank at high tide. A pin had worked out of a shackle.

A mooring can often be the cheapest solution, with another minor advantage in that the boat swings around, instead of sitting at the same angle to the sun and weather at all times, thus weathering evenly. You must be sure of your tackle at all times or you won't sleep well at night, and you have the nuisance of needing a dinghy or launch service to get aboard.

14

〰〰〰〰〰〰〰〰〰〰〰〰〰〰〰〰〰〰〰〰〰

On the Water

This is a book about buying boats, not operating them, and as mentioned in the previous chapter there are a host of how-to books available, plus the free instruction pamphlets issued by the Coast Guard and state agencies, as well as the education courses offered by the U.S. Power Squadrons and U.S. Coast Guard Auxiliary. However, I can't leave you with your new boat without a brief rundown of the basics of safety and good seamanship. Many people do buy boats and unfortunately start using them without realizing that there are such things, that there are rules of the road and equipment requirements, and that some boats are unsuitable for some conditions.

The most important single safety factor is simple common sense. It is common sense to know your limitations and then do something about them, and it is common sense to make sure that you have the proper equipment, that you have enough fuel for the passage you are making, and that you have checked the weather. You are afloat to enjoy yourself, and it is a shame to spoil the pleasure by not operating safely and properly.

Here are some of the elemental points in boating safety.

Safety Tips

NEVER OVERLOAD A BOAT
The single biggest cause of boating accidents is capsizing because of overloading small boats. Most small boats have a rated capacity indicated on a manufacturer's plate, and it should never be exceeded.

NEVER OVERPOWER A BOAT
Small boats are also rated for horsepower capacity, and to exceed it is asking for an accident. A boat that is seaworthy and easy to handle and control when properly powered can become a lethal monster with too much power.

DISTRIBUTE WEIGHT CORRECTLY
A frequent cause of capsizing in small open boats is a violent move by an occupant, such as jumping up suddenly when a fish strikes. In bad weather don't let everyone crowd in one part of the boat to avoid rain or spray, unbalancing the boat and inviting a capsize or swamping. It gives me the shakes to see boats go blithely by on a crowded waterway with youngsters sitting up at the bow on a curved, slippery deck, their feet dangling over the edge. They are probably obstructing the driver's view, a sudden big wake from a passing boat or a quick turn could throw them off under the boat, or they could be injured in a collision.

HANDLE FUEL CAREFULLY
Follow safety procedures while fueling, especially with gasoline. Do not smoke, and ground the edge of the fuel hose nozzle by holding it against the edge of the tank intake to prevent static electricity sparks from jumping across. Be careful of spills, especially into the bilge. Always

check the bilge for gas fumes after fueling and each time before starting the motor.

KNOW YOUR FUEL CAPACITY

Novices often head offshore with enough fuel for the mileage they expect to cover but not enough to take care of a weather change. What would be easy mileage in smooth water becomes too long a trip when wind and sea kick up from ahead later in the day. Capacity should be calculated in hours of operation, with an allowance for slowing down in adverse weather.

CHECK THE WEATHER

Get to know the typical weather patterns of an area. After-noon sea breezes can change mild-looking water into a rough and difficult stretch. Know the usual bearing for afternoon thunderstorms. On our river we have to beware if thunderheads build over a certain steeple on a hill to the northwest. Where thunderstorms are generally ex-pected, as on the west coast of Florida in summer, plan to be finished with your day afloat before the usual hour for the squalls. A radio to pick up the government weather frequencies is inexpensive and a good investment, and many local radio stations specialize in boating reports at certain times of day. Get to know the ones where you are.

KEEP A NAVIGATIONAL CHECK

Always know where you are. Have charts aboard and use them while under way. Check buoys or markers as you pass them so that you always have a good check on your position. Fog or a squall could suddenly reduce visibility and you would be completely lost. Even in bright fair weather and unlimited visibility, keep up the habit. If you suffer a breakdown and need help, it is good to know your position.

Reading charts is part of the fun of boating, and they can tell you a great deal. Laying off courses and distances can be a good challenge for youngsters or guests. If you have a depth recorder, you can also get a position check by following the bottom contour.

We have a constant reminder at home of how careless some boat operators can be about buoys and markers. There is a side channel that leads to a small inlet right near our pier. The channel comes to within 100 yards of the pier and then makes a 90-degree turn to starboard into the inlet, and there are flats and 1-foot shallows just beyond the turn. Time after time, boats come charging up the channel, fail to make the turn, and end up on the flats with a roar and a splash. One glimpse at a chart would show that there is no passage.

IF BAD WEATHER STRIKES

Try to avoid getting caught, but sometimes, even with good planning, your luck runs out. In a sailboat the first item of business is naturally to reduce sail. In a power-boat you may be able to run for shelter. If you are caught in heavy seas, keep the crew weight centered and low in the boat. Reduce speed and keep the bow to the wind and waves. In larger boats it may be best to run before the waves if there is plenty of sea room, but this can lead to steering difficulties, and it is not a good idea in outboard boats with low transoms. Never let the boat wallow in the trough of waves. Be prepared for pumping or bailing. In some cases you might be able to anchor, but this depends on the depth of the water and the size of the waves.

In fog or poor visibility the wind direction, which should have been known before the trouble started, might be a reference if you become disoriented. Even the smallest boat should have a compass aboard, and be sure to keep tools, knives, nonaluminum cans, and other metals away from it. Check it out in good weather to make sure it is still reliable.

LIFE JACKETS

Always have life jackets available, and require that they be worn at all times by children and nonswimmers. We made our children pass a 10-minute swimming test before they were allowed to go without jackets on our boats, and even then we put them on in rough going. Don't hesitate to require them for all hands if conditions call for it.

As I've already said, common sense is the key element and all the above are simply based on it. There is no need for fear and uncertainty on a boat if a positive attitude toward safety has been taken from the beginning.

Operations

While this is not an operator's manual, there are some points that should be mentioned as part of our capsule rundown. Getting afloat is the only way to gain experience, but the common-sense approach and an awareness of variables that affect boat operation can make getting that experience pleasanter and more meaningful.

Remember that you are in an element, not just on it (unless you are racing a 3-point hydroplane), and that a combination of forces is always at work on the boat. One of the joys of operating a boat under power or sail is to understand these forces, to work with them, and to make them work for you when possible. The key to sailing is, of course, making the wind work for you. This is the sport's fascination and its endless allure. In a powerboat the interplay is subtler and not as obvious. The boat's engine does most of the work, but the forces are there to be understood and used just the same.

WIND

It may sound ridiculously obvious, but you should always know where the wind is blowing from. This is one of the major confusions for a novice afloat, but it is vital knowledge at all times and in just about every maneuver. It is the first thing to know in a sailboat, which should have light telltales in the rigging. A powerboat skipper should always be aware of it, too. Learn to read signs that tell you wind direction, both near you and those at a distance from the boat, forecasting a change for you. Faraway flags, smokestacks, cloud movement, wave direction, all can be used. (You can even wet your finger and hold it up in the air.)

Remember that the wind across the deck of a boat in motion is always an apparent wind, a combination of the true wind and the movement of the boat. It is simple to understand that should you be on the open deck of an ocean liner going at 25 knots into a head wind of 25 knots, you are in an apparent wind of 50 and would be in 0 apparent wind if the course were reversed. It becomes a bit harder to grasp when the wind is at an angle to the boat's course, but the principle is the same.

CURRENT

Know when there is a current under you, as this always has an effect on the boat. It is especially important in docking maneuvers, anchoring, or picking up a mooring. In coastal waters the tide is always doing something, and inland waters have their own currents. Rivers are obvious, but lakes can have wind-generated currents that are a bit more mysterious and are not predictable like the tides of the ocean.

Check fixed objects like stakes, moorings, lobster pots, moored boats, and buoys to read the current past them. Even a 1-knot current can make quite a fuss around a fixed object. Always make use of what current there is in your maneuvers. In docking, anchoring, and picking up moorings, head into the current to reduce your speed and get added control. When wind and current are opposed, this can be a real problem in a sailboat, and you will have to estimate which is stronger and having more effect. In a deep-hulled boat current can have a strong effect, while light, high boats are more affected by the wind. When heading across a current, always allow for its sideways push. If you point your bow at something on the other side of a current, you won't end up at it. You will have to head up the current at an angle.

ANCHORING

Nothing shows up a novice as quickly as the handling of lines, whether it be anchoring or coming alongside. When anchoring, have the line coiled and ready to run free, not all in a tangle. Bring the boat to a stop, headed into wind and/or current, whichever is going to affect you more, at the exact spot where you want the anchor to hit the bottom, making sure there is room to swing in a 360-degree circle without fouling another boat by the time you have let your anchor line out. Then let the anchor go by easing it over the bow, not tossing it like an Olympic shot-putter, with the line running through your cupped hands. The boat should be going slowly backward by the time the anchor hits bottom, and the line should be let out to about 6 times the depth of water, as a general rule in normal conditions, perhaps a bit less in crowded areas. Let the boat drop back until almost all the scope you want has run out, then snub the line and see if the anchor is holding. The line should grow taut if it is. You can also watch the stern of the boat. The hull will have been drifting backward at a slight angle. When the anchor takes hold, the stern will start to swing, and will thereafter swing slowly back and forth while the anchor is holding. Once sure that the anchor is set, let off the rest of the required scope and make it fast to the proper cleat. It is often wise to put antichafe material like rags or a piece of rubber around the anchor line where it passes through the bow chock. Pick a range onshore of two trees in line, a tree and a house, or the like, so that you can check whether you are dragging.

In weighing anchor, use the engine to move up on the anchor, taking in the line as the boat moves forward. Power can also be used to break a well-set anchor free by going a bit ahead of the spot. Be sure to keep the anchor from gouging the topsides, and clean it off before bringing it aboard.

DOCKING

It is usually best to bring the boat alongside a docking space at a slight angle with the bow in, again using current and/or wind to best advantage. Have docking lines ready to run and free of tangles at bow and stern. Get the bowline ashore first and make it fast at an angle leading forward from the bow, then make the stern line fast, also at an angle aft of the stern. If you are staying for a time, and there is likely to be fore-and-aft motion of the boat, rig lines from the bow back along the hull to a point on the land near the stern and forward from the stern to a point near the bow. These are called springlines and can be used for bringing the boat in closer and for getting away from the dock. A slight push of power ahead while the bow spring is still attached will kick the stern out so that it is clear for backing away. Rig fenders from the boat's rail if the dock is rough and not protected.

In maneuvers under power, keep boat speed low but don't hesitate to use quick, short bursts of good power to swing a stern, back down, or turn in a tight space. A sudden rush of water against the propeller will be more effective than timidly applied power. Just keep the bursts short enough so that boat speed doesn't build up. Before approaching a slip, pier, or mooring, it is a wise precaution to check your controls. Test neutral and reverse.

KNOTS

You might have seen a knot board or a booklet from a rope company showing hundreds of knots, bends, splices, and the like. Marlinespike seamanship, as this is called, is a fascinating hobby and there are whole books on the subject. For this brief rundown, I recommend that you become familiar with a square knot, clove hitch, two half hitches and a bowline, and that you know how to cleat a line properly so that it doesn't jam. This repertoire will take care of just about every situation normally encountered.

STOWAGE

Stow your lines in coils in a locker that is readily accessible so that one can be broken out in an emergency all ready for use and not in a tangle.

In general, every item aboard any boat should have its proper stowage space, and it should be returned there immediately after use so that it can be located again right away. This applies to everything from lines, fenders, anchor, and life jackets right down to tools, spares, first-aid kit, and suntan lotion.

All these do's and don't's are not intended as a negative approach to boat owning and operation. Owning a boat and using her can be a tremendously rewarding pastime if the mechanics are carried out properly. And I certainly hope you get as much enjoyment out of the right boat for you as I have out of mine.

Appendix A

U.S. Coast Guard Equipment Requirements

EQUIPMENT	CLASS A (Less than 16 feet)	CLASS 1 (16 feet to less than 26 feet)	CLASS 2 (26 feet to less than 40 feet)	CLASS 3 (40 feet to not more than 65 feet)
BACKFIRE FLAME ARRESTER	1 approved device on each carburetor of all gasoline engines installed after April 25, 1940, except outboard motors			
VENTILATION	At least 2 ventilator ducts fitted with cowls or their equivalent for the purpose of properly and efficiently ventilating the bilges of every engine and fuel-tank compartment of boats constructed or decked over after April 25, 1940, using gasoline or other fuel of a flashpoint less than 110° F			
BELL	None*	None*	One, which when struck produces a clear, bell-like tone with a full, round sound	
LIFESAVING DEVICES	1 approved life preserver, buoyant vest, buoyant cushion, ring buoy, or special-purpose water-safety buoyant device for each person on board or being towed on water skis, etc.		1 approved life preserver or ring buoy for each person on board	

WHISTLE	None*	1 hand, mouth, or power operated, audible at least ½ mile	1 hand or power operated, audible at least 1 mile	1 power operated, audible at least 1 mile

PORTABLE FIRE EXTINGUISHER

When NO fixed fire extinguishing system is installed in machinery space(s)	At least 1 B-1-type, approved portable fire extinguisher (not required on outboard motorboat less than 26 feet in length and not carrying passengers for hire if the construction of such motorboats will not permit the entrapment of explosive or flammable gases or vapors)	At least 2 B-1-type, approved portable fire extinguishers; or at least 1 B-11-type, approved portable fire extinguisher	At least 3 B-1-type, approved portable fire extinguishers; or at least 1 B-1-type *plus* 1 B-11-type, approved portable fire extinguisher
When fixed fire extinguishing system is installed in machinery space(s)	None	At least 1 B-1-type, approved portable fire extinguisher	At least 2 B-1-type, approved portable fire extinguishers; or at least 1 B-11-type, approved portable fire extinguisher

* Not required by the Motorboat Act of 1940; however, the "rules of the road" require these vessels to sound proper signals.

Measuring for "Class"

For determining "class," the length of a boat is the distance measured from end to end over the deck excluding sheer. It means a straight-line measurement of the overall length from the foremost part of the vessel to the aftermost part of the vessel, measured parallel to the centerline. Bowsprits, bumpkins, rudders, outboard motors and brackets, and similar fittings or attachments are not to be included in the measurement.

For additional information see "Recreation Boating Guide" (CG-340) or inquire at any Coast Guard Marine Inspection office.

Backfire Flame Arresters

Flame arresters are not required on gasoline inboard engines installed prior to April 25, 1940. Installations of backfire flame arresters made before November 9, 1952, need not meet the latest requirements of approval and may be continued in use as long as they are in good condition. Automotive air breathers and containers with steel wool, however, are not acceptable. Engines installed after November 19, 1952, must have a Coast Guard–approved flame arrester fitted to the carburetor or bear a label indicating that the Coast Guard has approved the use of that engine without an arrester.

To meet the requirements, flame arresters must have flame-tight connections, clean elements, no separation of grid elements which would permit flames to bypass the grid elements, and be Coast Guard approved. The flame arrester's name and model number can be compared to the listing in the "Equipment List Booklet" (CG-190) or the arrester will have a Coast Guard approval number on the grid housing.

Exceptions are (1) engines accepted for use without a flame arrester and so labeled by the U.S. Coast Guard, and (2) situations where attachments to the air-intake system or the location of the engine will disperse backfire flame to open atmosphere clear of the vessel.

Lifesaving Devices

LIFE PRESERVERS

Kapok, fibrous glass, or unicellular plastic foam is used as flotation material in life preservers. They are either of the jacket or bib design and are acceptable for use on all types of motorboats and vessels. Adult sizes for persons 90 pounds and over and child sizes for those less than 90 pounds are available. Coast Guard–approved life preservers bear markings showing flotation material used, size, and U.S. Coast Guard approval number. All Coast Guard–approved life preservers manufactured after 1949 are Indian orange.

BUOYANT VESTS

Coast Guard–approved buoyant vests use the same flotation materials as life preservers but may be any color. Approved buoyant vests come in three sizes: adult, child medium, and child small. Weight ranges of the child sizes are included in the Coast Guard approval markings. It should be noted that buoyant vests provide less buoyancy than life preservers do. They are not acceptable on motorboats 40 feet in length and over or on vessels carrying passengers for hire.

BUOYANT CUSHIONS

Buoyant cushions approved by the Coast Guard contain kapok, fibrous glass, or unicellular plastic foam. They come in a variety of sizes and shapes and may be any color.

Cushions are not acceptable on motorboats 40 feet in length and over or on vessels carrying passengers for hire.

Approved buoyant cushions are marked on the side (gusset) with the Coast Guard approval number and other information concerning the cushion and its use. Buoyant cushions are intended for grasping and should never be worn on the back.

Ring buoys

Ring life buoys can be made of cork, balsa wood, or unicellular plastic foam and are available in 30-, 24-, and 20-inch sizes. Their covering is either canvas or specially surfaced plastic foam. All buoys are fitted with a grab line and may be colored either white or orange.

Cork and balsa-wood ring buoys must bear two markings, the manufacturer's stamp and the Coast Guard inspector's stamp. Plastic-foam ring buoys bear only a nameplate marking.

Special-purpose water-safety buoyant devices

These are manufactured in many designs and strengths depending on the intended special purpose, such as waterskiing, hunting, racing, etc.

Special-purpose devices include those to be worn and those to be grasped. They are acceptable on Classes A, 1, and 2 motorboats not carrying passengers for hire. Devices to be worn are available in adult and child sizes. All special-purpose devices show U.S. Coast Guard Approval Number E25/160.064 . . . , and include instructions on use and care and other necessary information. The devices intended for grasping also are marked: "Warning—do not wear on back."

Fire Extinguishers

Each fire extinguisher is classified, by letter and number, according to the type of fire it may be expected to extinguish and the size of the extinguisher. The letter indicates the type of fire: "A" for fires in ordinary combustible materials; "B" for gasoline, oil, and grease fires; "C" for fires in electrical equipment. Extinguishers approved for motorboats are portable, of either B-I or B-II classification.

FIRE EXTINGUISHERS

CLASSIFICATION (type-size)	FOAM (minimum gallons)	CARBON DIOXIDE (minimum pounds)	DRY CHEMICAL (minimum pounds)	FREON (minimum pounds)
B-I	1¼	4	2	2½
B-II	2½	15	10	—

Carbon-tetrachloride extinguishers and others of the toxic, vaporizing-liquid type such as chlorobromomethane are not approved and are not accepted as required fire extinguishers.

Approved types of fire extinguishers are identified by any of the following:

a. Make and model number. Check markings on nameplate against listing under company's name in the "Formerly Approved" section of the "Equipment Lists Booklet" (CG-190).

b. "Marine Type" marking. Check nameplate marking on Underwriters' Laboratories, Inc., listing manifest showing the words, "Marine Type USCG" followed by the Coast Guard classification such as "B-I," "B-II."

c. Coast Guard approval number. Check for marking of Coast Guard approval number on nameplate. Fire extinguishers manufactured after January 1, 1965, will be marked, "Marine Type USCG Type— Size— Approval No. 162-028. . . ."

Stored-pressure dry-chemical extinguishers manufactured after June 1, 1965, that have the propellant gases and extinguishing agent in the same bottle must have a visual pressure indicator—a pressure gauge or similar device that shows the state of internal-pressure charge.

Dry-chemical extinguishers manufactured prior to June 1, 1965, without pressure-indicating device are still acceptable if (1) inspection record shows weight check within the past 6 months; (2) weight is within $1/4$ ounce of weight stamped on container; (3) external seals or disk in neck are intact; and (4) there is no evidence of damage, use, or leaking.

Outboard Motorboats

In the case of outboard motorboats, the requirements for safety equipment must be met as specified for the general classes of motorboats of identical length, with the exception of the requirements of carburetor flame arrester. Those outboard motorboats with portable or permanent fuel tanks contained in a closed compartment must have two ducts, fitted with cowls or their equivalent, which will allow for the entrance of fresh air as well as the exhaust of fuel vapors.

Outboard motorboats less than 26 feet in length and not carrying passengers for hire need not carry fire extinguishers if the construction of such motorboats will not permit the entrapment of explosive or flammable gases or vapors.

Fire extinguishers must be carried in all boats that have: (1) closed compartments under thwarts and seats wherein portable fuel tanks may be stored, (2) double bottoms not sealed to the hulls or that are not completely filled with flotation material, (3) closed living spaces, (4) closed stowage compartments in which combustible or flammable materials are stowed, (5) permanently installed fuel tanks.

The following conditions do not *in themselves* require that fire extinguishers be carried: (1) bait wells, (2) glove compartments, (3) buoyant flotation material, (4) open-slatted flooring, (5) ice chests.

Appendix B   Partial NAYRU Equipment Lists for Offshore Racers

Structural Features

Hatches, companionways, and ports must be essentially watertight, that is, capable of being strongly and rigidly secured. Cockpit companionways, if extended below main-deck level, must be capable of being blocked off to main-deck level.

Cockpits must be structurally strong, self-bailing, and permanently incorporated as an integral part of the hull. They must be essentially watertight, that is, all openings to the hull below the main-deck level must be capable of being strongly and rigidly secured.

Cockpit drains must be adequate to drain cockpit quickly but with a combined area (after allowance for screens if attached) of not less than the equivalent of 2 1-inch (2.5-centimeter) diameter drains. Yachts built after January 1, 1972, must have drains with a combined area (after allowance for screens if attached) of not less than the equivalent of 4 ¾-inch (2-centimeter) drains.

Storm coverings for all windows more than 2 square feet in area.

Sea cocks or valves on all through-hull openings below LWL, except integral deck scuppers, shaft log, speed indicators, depth finders, and the like, however a means of closing such openings when necessary to do so shall be provided. Soft wood plugs, tapered and of various sizes.

Lifelines and pulpits. Fixed bow pulpit (forward of headstay) and stern pulpit (unless lifelines are arranged as to adequately substitute for a stern pulpit). Pulpits and stanchions must be through-bolted or welded, and the bases thereof must not be farther inboard from the edge of the working deck than 5 percent of B max. or 6 inches (15 centimeters), whichever is greater. The head of a stanchion must not be angled from the point of its attachment to the hull at more than 10 degrees from vertical. Taut double lifelines, with upper lifeline or wire at a height of not less than 2 feet (60 centimeters) above the working deck, to be permanently supported at intervals of not more than 7 feet (2.15 centimeters). A taut lanyard of synthetic rope may be used to secure lifelines, provided that when in position its length does not exceed 4 inches (10 centimeters). Lower lifelines need not extend through the bow pulpit. Lifelines need not be affixed to the bow pulpit if they terminate at, or pass through, adequately braced stanchions 2 feet (60 centimeters) above the working decks, set inside of and overlapping the bow pulpit, provided that the gap between the upper lifeline and the bow pulpit shall not exceed 6 inches (15 centimeters).

Yachts under 21-foot rating may be equipped as in paragraph above, but with a single taut lifeline not less than 18 inches (45 centimeters) above the working deck, and a bow pulpit and a stern pulpit (unless lifelines are arranged as to adequately substitute for a stern pulpit) to the same height. If the lifeline is at any point more than 22 inches (56 centimeters) above the rail cap, a second intermediate lifeline must be fitted. The bow pulpit may be fitted abaft the forestay with its bases secured at any points on deck, but a point on its upper rail must be within 16 inches (40 centimeters) of the forestay on which the foremost headsail is hanked.

Accommodations

Toilet, permanently installed.

Bunks, permanently installed.

Cooking stove, permanently installed with safe and accessible fuel shutoff control.

Galley facilities, including sink.

Water tanks, permanently installed and capable of dividing the water supply into at least two separate containers.

General Equipment

Fire extinguishers, readily accessible and of the type and number required by the country of registry, provided there be at least one in yachts fitted with an engine or stove.

Bilge pumps, at least two, manually operated, one of which must be operable with all cockpit seats and all hatches and companionways closed.

Anchors, two with cables except yachts rating under 21 feet, which shall carry at least one such anchor and cable.

Flashlights, water resistant, one of which is suitable for signaling, with spare batteries and bulbs.

First-aid kit and manual.

Foghorn.

Radar reflector.

Set of international code flags and international code book.

Shutoff valves on all fuel tanks.

Navigation Equipment

Compass, marine type, properly installed and adjusted.
Spare compass.
Charts, light list, and piloting equipment.
Sextant, tables, and accurate timepiece.
Radio direction finder.
Lead line or echo sounder.
Speedometer or distance-measuring instrument.
Navigation lights, to be shown as required by the International Regulations for Preventing Collision at Sea, mounted so that they will not be masked by sails or the heeling of the yacht.

Emergency Equipment

Spare running lights and power source.
Special storm sail(s) capable of taking the yacht to windward in heavy weather.
Heavy-weather jib and reefing equipment for mainsail.
Emergency steering equipment.
Tools and spare parts, including a hacksaw.
Yacht's name on miscellaneous buoyant equipment, such as life jackets, oars, cushions, etc. Portable sail number.
Marine radio transmitter and receiver with minimum transmitter power of 25 watts. If the regular antenna depends upon the mast, an emergency antenna must be provided.
Radio receiver capable of receiving weather bulletins.

Safety Equipment

Life jackets, one for each crew member.
Whistles (referee type) attached to life jackets.
Safety belt (harness type), one for each crew member.
Life raft(s) capable of carrying the entire crew and meet-

ing the following requirements: must be carried on deck (not under a dinghy) or in a special stowage opening immediately to the deck containing life raft(s) only; must be designed and used solely for saving life at sea; must have at least two separate buoyancy compartments, each of which must be automatically inflatable; each raft must be capable of carrying its rate capacity with one compartment deflated; must have a canopy to cover the occupants; must have been inspected, tested, and approved within the last two years by the manufacturer or other competent authority; and must have the following equipment appropriately secured to each raft.

1 sea anchor or drogue
1 bellows, pump, or other means for maintaining inflation of air chambers
1 signaling light
3 hand flares
1 bailer
1 repair kit
2 paddles
1 knife
1 rescue quoit and line
emergency water and rations to accompany raft

Life ring(s). At least one more horseshoe-type life ring equipped with a whistle (referee type), dye marker, a high-intensity water light, and a pole and flag. The pole is to be attached to the ring with 25 feet (8 meters) of floating line and is to be a length and so ballasted that the flag will fly at least 8 feet (2.45 meters) off the water.

Distress signals to be stowed in a waterproof container, and meeting the following requirements for each category, as indicated:
12 red parachute flares

4 white parachute flares
4 red hand flares
4 white hand flares

Heaving line, 50-foot (16-meter) minimum length, floating-type line readily accessible to cockpit.

Index